Mike McGrath

JavaScript

fifth edition

In easy steps is an imprint of In Easy Steps Limited
16 Hamilton Terrace · Holly Walk · Leamington Spa
Warwickshire · United Kingdom · CV32 4LY
www.ineasysteps.com

5th Edition

In Easy Steps Limited supports The Forest Stewardship Council (FSC),
the leading international forest certification organisation. All our titles
that are printed on Greenpeace approved FSC certified paper carry the
FSC logo.

MIX
Paper from
responsible sources
FSC **FSC® C020837**
www.fsc.org

Printed and bound in the United Kingdom

ISBN 978-1-84078-570-8

Contents

The creation of this book has been for me, Mike McGrath, an exciting personal journey in discovering how JavaScript can be implemented in today's web browsers with HTML5. It has been fascinating to discover how the modern Document Object Model (DOM) is implemented by Internet Explorer, Firefox, Google Chrome, Safari, and Opera. All the examples I have given in this book demonstrate JavaScript features that are presently supported by Internet Explorer and most other leading web browsers and the screenshots illustrate the actual results produced by the listed code. I truly believe that now, more than ever, authors can integrate JavaScript functionality with HTML5 content markup and CSS presentation to produce stunning interactive web pages.

Conventions in this book

In order to clarify the code listed in the steps given in each example I have adopted certain colorization conventions. Those parts of the JavaScript language itself are colored blue, like this:

document.addEventListener

Variable and function names specified by the script author are colored red, like this:

var myVariable ;

function myFunction () { }

Literal content of numeric or text string value is colored black, like this:

var myNumber = 7 ;

var myString = "JavaScript in easy steps" ;

Comments are colored green, like this:

// Statements to be executed go here.

Additionally, in order to identify each source code file described in the steps a colored icon and the file name appears in the margin alongside the steps, such as these:

page.html   script.js   style.css   vector.svg   string.txt   data.xml

Grabbing the source code

For convenience I have placed all the source code files and associated files featured in this book into a single ZIP archive file, arranged in folders numbered to match the chapter numbers. You can obtain the complete archive by following these easy steps:

1 Browse to **http://www.ineasysteps.com**, then navigate to the Free Resources tab and choose the Downloads section

2 Find JavaScript in easy steps, 5th edition in the list, then click on the hyperlink entitled All Code Examples to download the archive

3 Now extract the archive contents to any convenient location on your computer

Undoubtedly JavaScript and HTML5 provide significant new creative possibilities in web page authoring – as I trust my examples demonstrate. I sincerely hope you enjoy discovering how JavaScript can be used to create stunning interactive web pages in today's latest web browsers as much as I did in writing this book.

Mike McGrath

1 Getting started

Welcome to the exciting world of JavaScript. This chapter demonstrates how to incorporate script within an HTML document and introduces JavaScript functions and variables.

Introduction

JavaScript is an object-based scripting language whose interpreter is embedded inside web browser software, such as Microsoft Internet Explorer, Mozilla Firefox, Opera and Safari. This allows scripts contained in a web page to be interpreted when the page is loaded in the browser to provide functionality and dynamic effects. For security reasons JavaScript cannot read or write files, with the exception of "cookie" files that store minimal data.

Created by Brendan Eich at Netscape, JavaScript was first introduced in December 1995, and was initially named "LiveScript". It was soon renamed, however, to perhaps capitalize on the popularity of Sun Microsystems' Java programming language – although it bears little resemblance.

Brendan Eich, creator of the JavaScript language.

Before the introduction of JavaScript, web page functionality required the browser to call upon "server-side" scripts, resident on the web server, where slow response could impede performance. Calling upon "client-side" scripts, resident on the user's system, overcame the latency problem and provided a superior experience.

JavaScript quickly became very popular but a disagreement arose between Netscape and Microsoft over its licensing – so Microsoft introduced their own version named "JScript". Although similar to JavaScript, the new JScript version had extended features and some differences that remain today. Recognizing the danger of fragmentation, the JavaScript language was standardized by the European Computer Manufacturers Association (ECMA) in June 1997 as "ECMAScript". This helped to stabilize core features but the name, sounding like some kind of skin disease, is not widely used and most people will always call the language "JavaScript".

The JavaScript examples in this book describe three key ingredients:

- **Language basics** – illustrating the mechanics of the language syntax, keywords, operators, structure, and built-in objects

- **Web page functionality** – illustrating how to use the browser's Document Object Model (DOM) to provide user interaction and to create Dynamic HTML (DHTML) effects

- **Rich internet applications** – illustrating the latest AJAX techniques to create responsive web based applications

Hot tip

The Document Object Model (DOM) is a hierarchical arrangement of objects representing the currently-loaded HTML document.

JavaScript keywords

Keywords:					
break	case	catch	continue	default	delete
do	else	false	finally	for	function
if	in	instanceof	new	null	return
switch	this	throw	true	try	typeof
var	void	while	with		

The words listed in the table above are all "keywords" that have special meaning in JavaScript and may not be used when choosing names in scripts. You should also avoid using any of the reserved words that are listed in the table below as they may be introduced in future versions of JavaScript:

Reserved words:				
abstract	boolean	byte	char	class
const	debugger	double	enum	export
extends	final	float	goto	implements
import	int	interface	long	native
package	private	protected	public	short
static	super	synchronized	throws	transient
volatile				

Other words to avoid when choosing names in scripts are the names of JavaScript's built-in objects and browser DOM objects:

Objects (Built-in):				
Array	Date	Math	Object	String

Objects (DOM):				
window	location	history	navigator	document
images	links	forms	elements	XMLHttpRequest

Don't forget

JavaScript is a case-sensitive language where, for example, **VAR**, **Var**, and **var** are regarded as different words – of these three only **var** is a keyword.

11

Beware

Notice that all built-in object names begin with a capital letter and must be correctly capitalized, along with the DOM's **XMLHttpRequest** object.

Including inline script

JavaScript code can be included in a web page by adding HTML **<script> </script>** tags, to enclose the script, and the opening tag must have a **type** attribute specifying the unique MIME type of "text/javascript" – to identify the element's contents as JavaScript.

An HTML **<script>** element may also include helpful code comments. The JavaScript engine ("parser") ignores everything between **/*** and ***/** characters, allowing multi-line comments, and ignores everything between **//** characters and the end of a line, allowing single-line comments – like this:

```
<script type = "text/javascript">

/* This is a multi-line comment that might describe the script's
purpose and provide information about the author and date. */

// This is a single line comment that might describe a line of code.

</script>
```

Optionally, alternative text can be provided, for occasions when JavaScript support is absent or disabled, by adding **<noscript> </noscript>** HTML tags to enclose an explanatory message.

The **<script>** element can appear anywhere within the HTML document's body section to include "inline" JavaScript code, which will be executed as the browser reads down the document. Additionally, inline JavaScript code can be assigned to any of the HTML event attributes, such as **onload, onmouseover**, etc, which will be executed each time that event gets fired by a user action.

HTML

inline.html

1. Create an HTML document and add a **<div>** element to its body section, in which to write from JavaScript, and assign its **id** attribute a value of "panel"
```
<body>
        <div id = "panel" > </div>
</body>
```

2. In the **<div>** element, insert a **<script>** element containing inline code to write a greeting in the panel
```
<script type = "text/javascript" >

// Dynamically write a text string as this page loads.
document.write( "Hello World!" ) ;

</script>
```

3 After the **<script>** element, insert a **<noscript>** element for alternative text when JavaScript support is absent
<noscript>JavaScript is Not Enabled!</noscript>

4 Now, add an attribute to call a JavaScript method whenever the document gets loaded into the browser
// Display a message dialog after the page has loaded.
<body onload = " window.alert('Document Loaded!') ; ">

5 Save the HTML document and disable JavaScript support in your browser, then open the web page to see the alternative text get written in the panel

6 Enable JavaScript support to see the inline script write the greeting in the panel and open a message dialog box

Beware

Text strings must be enclosed within quote characters. Nested inner strings should be surrounded by single quote characters to avoid conflict with the double quote characters that surround outer strings.

13

Hot tip

This example calls the **write()** method of the DOM **document** object, to write the string within its parentheses, then calls the **alert()** method of the DOM **window** object, to display the text string within its parentheses in a dialog box.

Calling head section script

Adding JavaScript functionality with inline **<script>** elements and assigning code to HTML event attributes throughout the body section of a document is perfectly legitimate but it intrudes on the structural nature of the HTML elements and does not make for easy code maintenance. It is better to avoid inline script and, instead, place the JavaScript statements inside a "function" block within a single **<script>** element in the head section of the HTML document – between the **<head> </head>** tags.

A function block begins with the JavaScript **function** keyword, followed by a function name and trailing parentheses. These are followed by a pair of **{ }** curly brackets (braces) to enclose the statements. So its syntax looks like this:

```
function function-name ( )
{
    // Statements to be executed go here.
}
```

Notice that spaces, carriage returns, and tabs are collectively known as "whitespace" and are completely ignored in JavaScript code so the function can be formatted for easy readability. Some script authors prefer to place the opening brace on the same line as the function name, others choose to vertically align brace pairs.

Typically, a function to execute statements immediately after the HTML document has loaded in the browser is named "init" – as it performs <u>init</u>ial tasks. This function can be called upon to execute the statements it contains by stating its name (including the trailing parentheses) to the **onload** attribute of the HTML **<body>** tag like this:

```
<body onload = "init()" >
```

This nominates the function to be called by the browser when the window has loaded. At this point a load "event" occurs. The function nominated by the **onload** attribute is consequently known as the "event handler" – as it responds to that event.

There are many events that can occur in a web page, such as the click event that occurs when the user clicks a button, and JavaScript functions can be specified as event handlers for each one – to respond to each event.

Hot tip

A JavaScript function simply contains a set of statements to be executed whenever that function gets called.

Don't forget

Finding a missing brace in a lengthy function block can be very difficult if brace pairs are not vertically aligned.

1 Create an HTML document then add a **<div>** element to its body section, with an **id** attribute value of "panel"
<div id = "panel" > </div>

head.html

2 In the head section of the document, insert a **<script>** element containing an "init" function block
<script type = "text/javascript" >

function init()
{
    // Statements to be executed go here.
}

</script>

3 In the function block, insert statements to write text in the panel and to display a message dialog
document.getElementById("panel").innerHTML =
"Hello... from a Head Section JavaScript Block!" ;

window.alert("Document Loaded!") ;

4 Now, add an atribute to the **<body>** element – to call the function when the document has loaded into the browser
<body onload = "init()" >

15

5 Save the HTML document then open it in a JavaScript-enabled browser to see the function write text content in the panel and open a message dialog box

Hot tip

This example calls the **getElementById()** method of the DOM **document** object, to reference the panel element, then writes content by assigning a text string to its **innerHTML** property.

head.html

Head Section Script

Hello... from a Head Section JavaScript Block!

Message from webpage

Document Loaded!

OK

100%

Embedding external script

Where it is desirable to create a single portable HTML document its functionality can be provided by a **<script>** element within the document's head section, as in the previous example, and styling can be provided by a **<style>** element within the head section.

Where portability is of no importance, greater efficiency can be achieved by creating external script and style files. For instance, all the examples in this chapter could employ the same single style file to create a border style around the panel element. Similarly, all HTML files throughout a website could employ a single script file to embed JavaScript functionality in each web page. Often the JavaScript file may be referred to as a "library" because it contains a series of behavioral functions which can be called from any page on that website.

Embedding an external JavaScript file in the head section of an HTML document requires an **src** attribute be added to the usual **<script>** tag to specify the path to the script file. Where the script file is located in the same directory as the HTML document this merely needs to specify its file name and file extension – typically JavaScript files are given a ".js" file extension. For example, you can embed a local JavaScript file named "local.js" like this:

```
<script type = "text/javascript" src = "local.js" > </script>
```

The separation of structure (HTML), presentation (Cascading Style Sheets), and behavior (JavaScript), is recommended by the WorldWideWeb Consortium (W3C) as it makes site maintenance much simpler and each HTML document much cleaner – and so easier to validate.

Using HTML event attributes, such as **onload**, **onmouseover**, etc, to specify behavior continues to intrude on the structural nature of the HTML elements and is not in the spirit of the W3C recommendation. It is better to specify the behaviors in JavaScript code contained in an external file so the HTML document contains only structural elements, embedding behaviors and styles from elements in the head section specifying their file locations. The technique of completely separating structure and behavior in this way creates unobtrusive JavaScript, which is considered to be "best practice" and is employed throughout the rest of this book.

W3C®

The W3C is the recognized body that oversees standards on the Web. See the latest developments on their informative website at **www.w3.org**.

Don't forget

Remember to add the closing **</script>** tag. It is required even though the element is empty.

16

1 Create an HTML document then add a **<div>** element to its body section, with an **id** attribute value of "panel"
<div id = "panel" > </div>

external.html

2 In the head section of the HTML document, insert an element to embed an external JavaScript file
<script type = "text/javascript" src = "external.js" > </script>

3 Open a plain text editor, like Windows Notepad, and add an "init" function to write content in the panel and to display a message dialog box
function init()
{
  document.getElementById("panel").innerHTML =
  "Hello... from an External JavaScript File!" ;

  window.alert("Document Loaded!") ;
}

external.js

4 Immediately after the function block add a statement to call the function when the HTML document has loaded
window.onload = init ;

5 Save the HTML document then open it in a JavaScript-enabled browser to see the function write text content in the panel and open a message dialog box

17

Beware

An error will occur if you include trailing parentheses after the function name when assigning a function to the **window.onload** property – just assign its name only.

Accelerating initialization

The **window.load** event that occurs when a web page has loaded in the browser window is only triggered when all dependent resources have been <u>fully</u> loaded – including styles and images. This means that statements contained in the initializing JavaScript function will not be executed until all resources have been loaded. Where the page includes large image files it must wait for these to finish loading before the JavaScript initialization can take place.

As there may be an undesirable initialization delay in waiting for the **window.load** event to be triggered modern web browsers have been made to recognize a "DOMContentLoaded" event that is triggered when just the HTML document and script have loaded – without waiting for external resources such as images. The JavaScript initialization function can therefore be nominated as the event handler to the DOMContentLoaded event, rather than to the load event, to accelerate initialization. This means that statements contained in the initializing JavaScript function will be executed as soon as the HTML document and script have loaded. Where the page includes large image files it need not wait for these to finish loading before the JavaScript initialization happens.

Nomination of the JavaScript initialization function as the event handler to the DOMContentLoaded event must be made in a different way to that for the **window.onload** event. It requires a statement to "listen" out for the DOMContentLoaded event. This uses the JavaScript **document.addEventListener()** function to specify a comma-separated list of three parameters within its parentheses. The parameters state in order the event to listen out for, the name of the event handler function to call when that event is triggered, and an event phase. In the case of page initialization the event to listen out for is "DOMContentLoaded", the event handler function is typically named **init**, and the desired "bubbling phase" is specified with the boolean Javascript keyword **false**. So the entire statement looks like this:

document.addEventListener("DOMContentLoaded" , init , false) ;

As it is generally preferable to initialize the web page at the earliest opportunity the DOMContentLoaded event is used to execute the examples in this book. Its advantage can be seen by displaying a message dialog box when each event is triggered and noting the order in which they appear.

① Create an HTML document that embeds an external
JavaScript file and has a "panel" element in its body

```
<script type = "text/javascript" src = "domload.js" >
</script>
<div id = "panel" > </div>
```

domload.html

② Open a plain text editor, like Windows Notepad, and add
a function to simply display a message dialog box

```
function loaded()
{
  window.alert( "Window Loaded" ) ;
}
```

domload.js

③ Next, add an "init" function to write content in the panel
and to also display a message dialog box

```
function init()
{
  document.getElementById( "panel" ).innerHTML =
  "Page Initialized" ;
  window.alert( "DOM Loaded" ) ;
}
```

④ After the function blocks add statements to call an
appropriate function when a event occurs

```
window.onload = loaded ;
document.addEventListener( "DOMContentLoaded", init, false ) ;
```

⑤ Save the script alongside the HTML document then
open the web page in a browser to see the message dialog
box and panel identify the event that occurs first

19

Beware

The **DOMContentLoaded**
event fires when just
the HTML document
has loaded whereas the
window.onload event
only fires when the
entire page, including
images, has loaded – but
you must include that
alternative if you are
trying out any of this
book's examples in an
older web browser.

Storing data in variables

A "variable" is a container, common to every scripting and programming language, in which data can be stored and retrieved later. Unlike the "strongly typed" variables in most other languages, which must declare a particular data type they may contain, JavaScript variables are much easier to use because they are "loosely typed" – so they may contain any type of data:

Data Type:	Example:	Description:
boolean	**true**	A true (1) or false (0) value
number	**100** **3.25**	An integer or A floating-point number
string	**"M"** **"Hello World!"**	A single character or A string of characters, with spaces
function	**init** **fido.bark**	A user-defined function or A user-defined object method
object	**fido** **document**	A user-defined object or A built-in object

A JavaScript variable is declared using the **var** keyword followed by a space and a name of your choosing, within certain naming conventions. The variable name may comprise letters, numbers, and underscore characters, but may not contain spaces or begin with a number. Additionally, you must avoid the JavaScript keywords, reserved words, and object names listed in the tables on page 11. The declaration of a variable in a script may simply create a variable to which a value can be assigned later, or may include an assignation to instantly "initialize" the variable with a value:

```
var myNumber ;                        // Declare a variable.
myNumber = 10 ;                       // Initialize a variable.
var myString = "Hello World!" ; // Declare and initialize a variable.
```

Multiple variables may be be declared on a single line too:

```
var i , j , k ;              // Declare 3 variables.
var num =10 , char = "C" ;  // Declare and initialize 2 variables.
```

Upon initialization, JavaScript automatically sets the variable type for the value assigned. Subsequent assignation of a different data type later in the script can be made to change the variable type. The current variable type can be revealed by the **typeof** keyword.

1 Create an HTML document that embeds an external JavaScript file and has a "panel" element in its body

```
<script type = "text/javascript" src = "variable.js" >
</script>
<div id = "panel" > </div>
```

variable.html

2 Open a plain text editor, like Windows Notepad, and add a function to execute after the document has loaded

```
function init()
{
  // Statements to be executed go here.
}
document.addEventListener( "DOMContentLoaded", init, false ) ;
```

variable.js

3 In the function block, insert statements to declare and intialize variables of different data types

```
var str = "Text Content in JavaScript" ;
var num = 100 ;
var bln = true ;
var fcn = init ;
var obj = document.getElementById( "panel" ) ;
```

Hot tip

The **typeof** returns a value of "undefined" for uninitialized variables.

21

4 Now, insert statements to write the variable values and data types into the panel

```
obj.innerHTML = str + " : " + typeof str ;
obj.innerHTML += "<br>" + num + " : " + typeof num ;
obj.innerHTML += "<br>" + bln + " : " + typeof bln ;
obj.innerHTML += "<br>init() : " + typeof fcn ;
obj.innerHTML += "<br>" + obj + " : " + typeof obj ;
```

5 Save the script alongside the HTML document then open the page in your browser to see the variable data

Hot tip

Notice how the + operator is used here to join (concatenate) parts of a string and with += to append strings onto existing strings.

Passing function arguments

Functions and variables are the key components of JavaScript.

A function may be called once or numerous times to execute the statements it contains. Those functions that belong to an object, such as **document.write()**, are known as "methods" – just to differentiate them from user-defined functions. Both have trailing parentheses that may accept "argument" values to be passed to the function for manipulation. For example, the text string value passed in the parentheses of the **document.write()** method that gets written into the HTML document.

The number of arguments passed to a function must match those specified within the parentheses of the function block declaration. For example, a user-defined function requiring exactly one argument looks like this:

```
function function-name ( argument-name )
{
  // Statements to be executed go here.
}
```

Multiple arguments can be specified as a comma-separated list:

```
function function-name ( argument-A , argument-B , argument-C )
{
  // Statements to be executed go here.
}
```

Like variable names, function names and argument names may comprise letters, numbers, and underscore characters, but may not contain spaces or begin with a number. Additionally, you must avoid the JavaScript keywords, reserved words, and object names listed in the tables on page 11.

Optionally, a function can return a value to the caller using the **return** keyword at the end of the function block. After a return statement has been made the script flow continues at the caller – so no further statements in the called function get executed. It is typical to return the result of manipulating passed argument values back to the caller:

```
function function-name ( argument-A , argument-B , argument-C )
{
  // Statements to be executed go here.

  return result ;
}
```

Hot tip

Just as object functions are known as "methods" their variables are known as "properties".

Don't forget

Multiple arguments must also be passed as a comma-separated list.

① Create an HTML document that embeds an external JavaScript file and has a "panel" element in its body
```
<script type = "text/javascript" src = "argument.js" >
</script>
<div id = "panel" > </div>
```

argument.html

② Open a plain text editor and add a function to execute after the HTML document has loaded
```
function init()
{
  // Statements to be executed go here.
}
document.addEventListener( "DOMContentLoaded", init, false ) ;
```

argument.js

③ In the function block, insert a statement that calls another user-defined function and passes it four argument values
```
document.getElementById( "panel" ).innerHTML =
        stringify( "JavaScript" , "In" , "Easy" , "Steps" ) ;
```

④ Next, insert a second statement that also calls the user-defined function, passing it four different argument values
```
document.getElementById( "panel" ).innerHTML+=
        stringify( "Written" , "By" , "Mike" , "McGrath" ) ;
```

⑤ Now, before the init function block, declare the function being called from the statements within the init function
```
function stringify( argA , argB , argC , argD )
{
  var str=argA+" "+argB+" "+argC+" "+argD+"<br>" ;
  return str ;
}
```

Beware

A function must have been declared before it can be called, so function declarations should appear first in the script.

⑥ Save the script alongside the HTML document then open the page in your browser to see the returned values

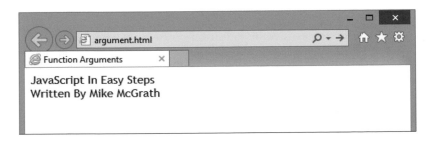

```
argument.html

Function Arguments

JavaScript In Easy Steps
Written By Mike McGrath
```

Recognizing variable scope

The extent to which a variable is accessible is called its "scope" and is determined by where the variable is declared:

● A variable declared inside a function block is only accessible to code within that same function block. This variable has "local" scope – it is only accessible locally within that function, so is known as a "local variable"

● A variable declared outside all function blocks is accessible to code within any function block. This variable has "global" scope – it is accessible globally within any function in that script so is known as a "global variable"

Local variables are generally preferable to global variables as their limited scope prevents possible accidental conflict with other variables. Global variable names must be unique throughout the entire script but local variable names only need be unique throughout their own function block – so the same variable name can be used in different functions without conflict.

scope.html

scope.js

1 Create an HTML document that embeds an external JavaScript file and has a "panel" element in its body
```
<script type = "text/javascript" src = "scope.js" >
</script>
<div id = "panel" > </div>
```

2 Open a plain text editor then declare and initialize a global variable
```
var global = "This is Worldwide Global news<hr>" ;
```

3 Add a function to execute after the HTML document has loaded
```
function init()
{
    // Statements to be executed go here.
}
document.addEventListener( "DOMContentLoaded", init, false ) ;
```

4 In the function block, declare and initialize a local variable then write the value of the global variable into the panel

```
var obj = document.getElementById( "panel" ) ;
obj.innerHTML = global ;
```

5 Now, in the function block call two other functions, passing the value of the local variable to each one

```
us( obj ) ;
eu( obj ) ;
```

Hot tip

Notice that the "local" variable names do not conflict because they are only visible within their respective function blocks.

6 Before the "init" function block, insert a function with one argument that initializes a local variable, then appends its value and that of the global variable into the panel

```
function us( obj )
{
  var local = "***This is United States Local news***<br>" ;
  obj.innerHTML += local ; obj.innerHTML += global ;
}
```

7 Before the init function block, insert another function with one argument that initializes a local variable, then appends its value and that of the global variable into the panel

```
function eu( obj )
{
  var local = "---This is European Local news---<br>" ;
  obj.innerHTML += local ; obj.innerHTML += global ;
}
```

8 Save the script alongside the HTML document then open the page in your browser to see the values of the global and local variables written by the functions

Don't forget

A variable can be declared without initialization, then assigned a value later in the script to initialize it.

Browser window — address bar: scope.html — tab title: Variable Scope

This is Worldwide Global news

*** This is United States Local news ***
This is Worldwide Global news

--- This is European Local news ---
This is Worldwide Global news

25

Summary

- JavaScript is a client-side, object-based, case-sensitive language whose interpreter is embedded in web browser software

- Variable names and function names must avoid the JavaScript keywords, reserved words, and object names

- For JavaScript code each opening HTML **<script>** tag must specify the MIME type of "text/javascript" to its **type** attribute

- Script blocks may include single-line and multi-line comments

- Each JavaScript statement must be terminated by a semi-colon

- Inline JavaScript code can be assigned to any HTML event attribute, such as **onload**, or enclosed within a **<script>** element in the document body section – but is best avoided

- All JavaScript code is best located in an external file whose path is specified to an **src** attribute of the **<script>** tag

- Unobtrusive JavaScript places all script code in an external file and can specify a function to the **DOMContentLoaded** event to set behaviors when the HTML document has loaded

- The **window.onload** event can be used to set behaviors for older browsers when the entire page content has loaded

- JavaScript variables are declared using the **var** keyword and can store any data type – boolean, number, string, function, or object

- JavaScript functions are declared using the **function** keyword and the function name must have trailing parentheses, followed by a pair of { } braces enclosing statements to execute

- A function declaration may specify arguments within its trailing parentheses that must be passed from its caller

- A value can be returned to the caller using the **return** keyword

- Unlike global variables declared in the main script body, local variables declared inside a function are only accessible from within that function

2 Performing operations

This chapter describes each of the basic JavaScript operators and demonstrates how they are used.

Doing arithmetic

The arithmetical operators commonly used in JavaScript are listed in the table below with the operation they perform:

Operator:	Operation:
+	Addition of numbers Concatenation of strings
–	Subtraction
*	Multiplication
/	Division
%	Modulus
++	Increment
– –	Decrement

Values specified in operation statements are called "operands". For example, in the statement 5 + 2 the + operator is supplied operand values of five and two.

Notice that the + operator performs two kinds of operation depending on the type of operands. Numeric operands are added to produce a sum total, whereas string operands are concatenated to produce a single joined string.

The % modulus operator divides the first operand by the second operand and returns the remainder. Dividing by two will return either one or zero to usefully determine whether the first operand is an odd number or an even number.

The ++ increment operator and -- decrement operator alter the value of a single operand by one and return the new value. These operators are most commonly used to count iterations of a loop and can be used in two different ways to subtly different effect. When placed before the operand (prefix) its value is immediately changed before the expression is evaluated. When placed after the operand (postfix) the expression is evaluated first then the value gets changed.

Hot tip

An example using the modulus operator to determine odd or even numbers can be found on page 37.

1 Create an HTML document that embeds an external script file and contains an element in which to write

```
<script type = "text/javascript" src = "arithmetic.js" >
</script>
<div id = "panel" > </div>
```

arithmetic.html

2 Create the JavaScript file with an "init" function to initialize variables using each of the arithmetic operators

```
function init()
{
  var sum = 80 + 20 ;   // Add two operands.
  var sub = sum - 50 ;  // Subtract 2nd operand from 1st.
  var mul = sum * 5 ;   // Multiply two operands.
  var div = sum / 4 ;   // Divide 1st operand by 2nd.
  var mod = sum % 2 ;   // Remainder after dividing by two.
  var inc = ++sum ;     // Immediately increment by one.
  var dec = --sum ;     // Immediately decrement by one.
}
document.addEventListener( "DOMContentLoaded", init, false ) ;
```

arithmetic.js

3 Next, in the function block, concatenate strings and each of the variable values into a single string variable

```
var str = "Sum: " + sum + "<br>Subtraction: " + sub ;
str += "<br>Multiplication: " + mul ;
str += "<br>Division: " + div + "<br>Modulus: " + mod ;
str += "<br>Increment: " + inc ;
str += "<br>Decrement: " + dec ;
```

4 Now, in the function block, write the string into the panel
`document.getElementById( "panel" ).innerHTML = str ;`

5 Save the script alongside the HTML document then open the page in a browser to see the result of each operation

```
arithmetic.html

Arithmetic Operations

Sum: 100
Subtraction: 50
Multiplication: 500
Division: 25
Modulus: 0
Increment: 101
Decrement: 100
```

Don't forget

The HTML **<noscript>** element that provides alternative text only detects whether the browser has JavaScript enabled or not. If JavaScript is disabled in the Firewall rather than in the browser then the JavaScript will not run and the content of the **<noscript>** tag will not be displayed.

Assigning values

The operators that are commonly used in JavaScript to assign values are all listed in the table below. All except the simple = assignment operator are shorthand forms of longer expressions so each equivalent is also given for clarity:

Operator:	Example:		Equivalent:
=	a = b		a = b
+=	a += b		a= (a + b)
−=	a −= b		a = (a − b)
*=	a *= b		a = (a * b)
/=	a /= b		a = (a / b)
%=	a %= b		a = (a % b)

It is important to think of the = operator as meaning "assign" rather than "equals" to avoid confusion with the === equality operator.

In the = example in the table the variable **a** gets assigned the value contained in variable **b** to become its new stored value.

The combined += operator is most useful and has been employed in previous examples to append a string onto an existing string. Numerically speaking, the += example in the table will add the value contained in variable **a** to that contained in variable **b** then assign the sum total to become the new value stored in variable **a**.

All other combined assignment operators work in a similar way to the += operator. They each perform the arithmetical operation on their two operands first, then assign the sum result of that operation to the first variable – so that becomes its new stored value.

Hot tip

The === equality operator compares values and is fully explained on page 32.

1 Create an HTML document that embeds an external
script file and contains an element in which to write
**<script type = "text/javascript" src = "assign.js" >
</script> <div id = "panel" > </div>**

assign.html

2 Create the JavaScript file with an "init" function to
initialize variables modified by each assignment operator

assign.js

```
function init()
{
  var msg = "JavaScript" ; msg += " Code" ; //Concatenate
  var flt = 7.5 ; flt += 2.25 ;      // Add and assign.
  var intA = 8 ; intA -= 4 ;         // Subtract and assign.
  var intB = 24 ; intB *= intA ;     // Multiply and assign.
  var intC = 24 ; intC /= intA ;     // Divide and assign.
  var intD = 24 ; intD %= intA ;     // Modulus and assign.
}
document.addEventListener( "DOMContentLoaded", init, false ) ;
```

3 Next, in the function block, concatenate strings and each
of the variable values into a single string variable

```
var str = "Add & assign string: " + msg ;
str += "<br>Add & assign float: " + flt ;
str += "<br>Subtract & assign: " + intA ;
str += "<br>Multiply & assign: " + intB ;
str += "<br>Divide & assign: " + intC ;
str += "<br>Modulus & assign: " + intD ;
```

4 Now, in the function block, write the string into the panel
document.getElementById("panel").innerHTML = str ;

5 Save the script alongside the HTML document then open
the page in a browser to see the result of each assignment

Comparing values

The operators that are commonly used in JavaScript to compare two values are all listed in the table below:

Operator:	Comparison:
===	Equality
!==	Inequality
>	Greater than
<	Less than
>=	Greater than or equal to
<=	Less than or equal to

The === equality operator compares two operands and will return a boolean **true** value if they are exactly equal, otherwise it will return a boolean **false** value. If the operands are identical numbers they are equal, if the operands are strings containing the same characters in the same positions they are equal, if the operands are boolean values that are both **true**, or both **false**, they are equal. Conversely the !== inequality operator returns true if the two operands are not equal, using the same rules as the === equality operator.

Equality and inequality operators are useful in comparing two values to perform "conditional branching", where the script will follow a particular direction according to the result.

The > greater than operator compares two operands and returns true if the first is greater in value than the second. The < less than operator makes the same comparison but returns true when the first is less in value than the second. Adding the = character after the > greater than operator or the < less than operator makes them also return true when the two operands are equal.

The > greater than and < less than operators are frequently used to test the value of a counter variable in a loop structure.

Hot tip

An example using the < less than operator in a loop structure can be found on page 49.

Beware

There is also a == equality operator and a != inequality operator, but these may produce unexpected results as they can perform type coercion. For example **true == 1** returns **true** wheareas **true === 1** returns **false**. Always use the three-character versions that do not perform type coercion.

① Create an HTML document that embeds an external script file and contains an element in which to write
```
<script type = "text/javascript" src = "compare.js" >
</script> <div id = "panel" > </div>
```

compare.html

② Create the JavaScript file with an "init" function to initialize a number of variables by each of the comparison operators
```
function init()
{
  var strA = "JavaScript" === "JAVASCRIPT" ;
  var strB = "JavaScript" === "JavaScript" ;
  var flt = 7.5 === 7.5 ;          // Equality test.
  var intA = 8 !== 8 ;             // Inequality test
  var intB = 24 > 12 ;            // Greater than test.
  var intC = 24 < 12 ;            // Less than test.
  var intD = 24 <= 24 ;           // Less than or equal test.
}
document.addEventListener( "DOMContentLoaded", init, false ) ;
```

compare.js

③ Next, in the function block, concatenate strings and each of the variable values into a single string variable
```
var str = "String equality test 1: " + strA ;
str += "<br>String equality test 2: " + strB ;
str += "<br>Float equality test: " + flt ;
str += "<br>Integer inequality test: " + intA ;
str += "<br>Greater than test: " + intB ;
str += "<br>Less than test: " + intC ;
str += "<br>Less than or equal test: " + intD ;
```

④ Now, in the function block, write the string into the panel
```
document.getElementById( "panel" ).innerHTML = str ;
```

⑤ Save the script alongside the HTML document then open the page in a browser to see the result of each comparison

Don't forget

JavaScript is case-sensitive, so character capitalization must match for compared strings to be equal.

```
compare.html                                    🔍 ⌂ ★ ⚙
Comparison Operations        ×
String equality test 1: false
String equality test 2: true
Float equality test: true
Integer inequality test: false
Greater than test: true
Less than test: false
Less than or equal test: true
```

Assessing logic

The three logical operators that can be used in JavaScript are listed in the table below:

Operator:	Operation:
&&	Logical AND
||	Logical OR
!	Logical NOT

The logical operators are typically used with operands that have a boolean value of **true** or **false** – or values that can convert to **true** or **false**.

The **&&** logical AND operator will evaluate two operands and return **true** only if both operands are themselves **true**. Otherwise the **&&** AND operator will return **false**. This is often used in conditional branching where the direction of the script is determined by testing two conditions. If both conditions are satisfied the script will follow a particular direction, otherwise it will follow a different direction.

Unlike the **&&** logical AND operator, which needs both operands to be **true**, the **||** logical OR operator will evaluate two operands and return **true** if either one of the operands is itself **true**. If neither operand is **true** then the **||** OR operator will return **false**. This is useful to have a script perform a certain action if either one of two test conditions are satisfied.

The third logical operator is the **!** logical NOT operator that is used before a single operand and it returns the inverse value of the operand . For example, if variable **a** had a **true** value then **!a** would return **false**. This is useful to "toggle" the value of a variable in successive loop iterations with a statement like **a=!a** so that the value is reversed on each iteration – like flicking a light switch on and off.

1 Create an HTML document that embeds an external script file and contains an element in which to write

```
<script type = "text/javascript" src = "logic.js" ></script>
<div id = "panel" > </div>
```

logic.html

2 Create the JavaScript file with an "init" function to initialize a number of variables using each logic operator

```
function init()
{
  var yes = true , no = false ;    // Initialize with booleans.
  var blnA = yes && yes ;          // Test if both are true.
  var blnB = yes && no ;           // Test if both are true.
  var blnC = no || yes ;           // Test if either is true.
  var blnD = no || no ;            // Test if either is true.
  var tog = !yes ;                 // Reverse the value.
}
document.addEventListener( "DOMContentLoaded", init, false ) ;
```

logic.js

3 Next, in the function block, concatenate strings and each of the variable values into a single string variable

```
var str = "Are both values true?: " + blnA + "<br>" ;
str += "Are both values true now?: " + blnB + "<br>" ;
str += "Is either value true?: " + blnC + "<br>" ;
str += "Is either value true now?: " + blnD + "<br>" ;
str += "Initial value: " + yes + "<br>" ;
str += "Toggled value: " + tog + "<br>" ;
```

4 Now, in the function block, write the string into the panel

```
document.getElementById( "panel" ).innerHTML = str ;
```

5 Save the script alongside the HTML document then open the page in a browser to see the result of each assessment

Examining conditions

Possibly the JavaScript author's favorite operator is the **?:** conditional operator. This operator evaluates a specified condition for a true or false value then executes one of two specified statements according to the result. Its syntax looks like this:

condition ? _if-true-do-this_ : _if-false-do-this_ ;

Where multiple actions are required to be performed, according to the result of the condition evaluation, each specified statement may be a function call to execute multiple statements in each function. For example, calling functions to execute multiple statements according to the boolean value of a "flag" variable like this:

flag === true ? doThis() : doThat() ;

In this example the **===** equality operator and **true** keyword are actually superfluous as operators that evaluate an expression for a boolean value automatically perform this assessment, so the example could be more simply stated as:

flag ? doThis() : doThat() ;

Alternatively the two statements specified to the conditional operator might assign a value to a variable according to the result of the condition evaluation like this:

flag ? str = "Go left" : str = "Go right" ;

While this is syntactically correct it can be more elegantly expressed by having the conditional operator assign an appropriate value to the variable in a single assignment statement like this:

str = flag ? "Go left" : "Go right" ;

Where the condition evaluates the parity of a numeric value the two statements can supply alternatives according to whether the evaluation determines the number to be even or odd.

1 Create an HTML document that embeds an external script file and contains an element in which to write
```
<script type = "text/javascript" src = "condition.js" >
</script> <div id = "panel" > </div>
```

condition.html

2 Create the JavaScript file with an "init" function to initialize a variable by the conditional operator and a further string variable
```
function init()
{
  var state = 7 > 5 ? "Greater" : "Smaller" ;
  var str = "7 is " + state + " than 5" ;
}
document.addEventListener( "DOMContentLoaded", init, false ) ;
```

condition.js

3 Next, in the function block, insert more conditional assignments and append to the string variable
```
state = 7 > 10 ? "Greater" : "Smaller" ;
        str += "<br>7 is " + state + " than 10" ;
state = 7 === 8 ? "Equal" : "Not Equal" ;
        str += "<br>7 is " + state + " to 8" ;
state = 7 % 2 === 0 ? "Even" : "Odd" ;
        str += "<br>7 is an " + state + " number" ;
```

4 Now, in the function block, write the string into the panel
```
document.getElementById( "panel" ).innerHTML = str ;
```

5 Save the script alongside the HTML document then open the page in your browser to see each conditional assignment

Hot tip

Notice how this example efficiently re-uses the **state** variable, rather than assign each result to a separate variable.

37

Setting precedence

JavaScript operators have different levels of priority to determine the order in which a statement containing multiple different operators gets evaluated – those with higher priority take precedence over those with lower priority. The table below lists each type of operator in order of highest to lowest priority from top to bottom of the table:

Operator:	Operation:	Priority:
* / %	Multiplication, Division, Modulus	Highest
+ –	Addition, Subtraction	
< <= => >	Comparison	
== !=	Equality	
&&	Logical AND	
||	Logical OR	
?:	Conditional	
= += –= *= /= %=	Assignment	Lowest

Hot tip

Make a habit of using parentheses to set the precedence order in which to evaluate expressions.

It is important to be aware of operator precedence to avoid unwanted results from statements containing multiple operators. For example, consider the following statement:

var sum = 9 + 12 / 3 ;

The evaluation first computes the division as its operator has higher priority than the addition operator, so the result is **13**. But you can set the precedence by enclosing an expression within parentheses so it will be evaluated first. In this case **(9 + 12) / 3** performs the addition first, so the result is **7**.

1 Create an HTML document that embeds an external script file and contains an element in which to write
<script type = "text/javascript" src = "priority.js" > </script> <div id = "panel" > </div>

priority.html

2 Create the JavaScript file with an "init" function to initialize a variable using default operator priority and a further string variable
```
function init()
{
  var sum = 2 * 9 + 12 / 3 ;  // Equivalent to (2*9) + (12/3).
  var str = "18 + 4 = " + sum ;
}
document.addEventListener( "DOMContentLoaded", init, false ) ;
```

priority.js

3 Next, in the function block, insert assignments with set precedence and append to the string variable
```
sum = ( ( 2 * 9 ) + 12 ) / 3 ;  // Equivalent to (18+12) / 3.
str += "<br>30 / 3 = " + sum ;

sum = ( 2 * ( 9 + 12 ) ) / 3 ;  // Equivalent to (2*21) / 3.
str += "<br>42 / 3 = " + sum ;

sum = 2 * ( 9 + ( 12 / 3 ) ) ;  // Equivalent to 2 * (9+4).
str += "<br>2 * 13 = " + sum ;
```

4 Now, in the function block, write the string into the panel
document.getElementById("panel").innerHTML = str ;

5 Save the script alongside the HTML document then open the page in a browser to see the result of each assignment

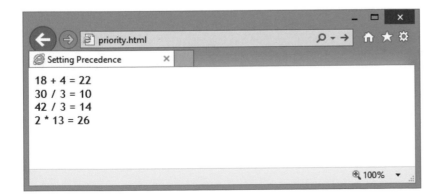

```
18 + 4 = 22
30 / 3 = 10
42 / 3 = 14
2 * 13 = 26
```

Don't forget

Where a statement contains nested expressions within parentheses the innermost expression gets evaluated first.

39

Summary

- Arithmetic operators are + add, – subtract, * multiply, / divide, % modulus, ++ increment, and – – decrement

- When the ++ increment or – – decrement operator prefixes the operand its value is changed immediately, but when they appear after the operand the expression is evaluated first

- The basic = assignment operator should not be confused with the === equality operator, which compares two operands

- Combined assignment operators +=, -=, *=, /=, and %=, each perform an arithmetic operation then assign its result

- The += operator is useful to append to an existing string

- Two operands can be compared for === equality, !== inequality, > greater-than value, or < less-than value

- The <= and >= combined comparison operators also return true when both operands are equal

- The logical && AND operator evaluates two operands and returns true when both operands are true, but the logical || OR operator returns true when either operand is true

- The logical ! NOT operator can prefix a single operand to return its inverse value

- Conditional operator ?: evaluates a condition for a true or false value then executes one of two specified statements according to the result

- Expressions being evaluated for a true or false value need not include === true as that assessment is made automatically

- Operator precedence can be set by enclosing an expression within parentheses to override the default operator priority

- Where a statement contains nested expressions within parentheses the innermost expression gets evaluated first

3 Controlling flow

This chapter demonstrates how to provide branches and loops to perform a variety of script tasks.

Branching with if

The progress of any script or computer program depends upon the evaluation of conditions to determine the direction of flow. Each evaluation may present one or more branches along which to continue according to the result of the evaluation.

In JavaScript the basic conditional test is performed with the **if** keyword to test a condition for a boolean value. When the result is true a statement following the evaluation will be executed, otherwise this is skipped and flow continues at the next subsequent statement. The syntax of an **if** statement demands that the condition to be tested is placed within parentheses after the **if** keyword and looks like this:

if (*condition*) *execute-this-statement-when-true* ;

An **if** statement may also specify multiple statements to be executed when the result is true by enclosing those statements within braces, like this:

```
if ( condition )
{
  execute-this-statement-when-true ;
  execute-this-statement-when-true ;
  execute-this-statement-when-true ;
}
```

The evaluation of a condition and the execution of actions according to its result simply reflects the real-life thought process. For example, the actions you might execute on a summer day:

```
var temperature = readThermometer() ;
var tolerable = 30 ;

if ( temperature > tolerable )
{
  turn_on_air-conditioning() ;
  get_a_cool_drink() ;
  stay_in_shade() ;
}
```

① Create an HTML document that embeds an external script file and contains an element in which to write

```
<script type = "text/javascript" src = "if.js" > </script>
<div id = "panel" > </div>
```

if.html

② Create the JavaScript file with an "init" function to initialize a variable and perform a conditional test of its value

```
function init()
{
  var flag = true ;
  if ( flag )
  { document.getElementById( "panel" ).innerHTML =
                                    "Power is On" ;

  }
}
document.addEventListener( "DOMContentLoaded", init, false ) ;
```

if.js

③ Next, in the function block, add two more conditional tests – one that will fail and one that will succeed

```
if ( 7 < 2 )
{
  document.getElementById( "panel" ).innerHTML +=
                                    "<br>Failure" ;

}

if ( 7 > 2 )
{
  document.getElementById( "panel" ).innerHTML +=
                                    "<br>Success" ;

}
```

④ Save the script alongside the HTML document then open the page in a browser to see the result of each test

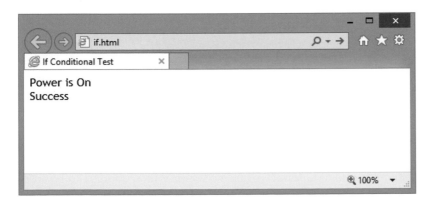

Branching alternatives

An **if** statement, which tests a condition for a boolean value and only executes its statements when the result is true, provides a single branch that the script may follow. An alternative branch that the script can follow when the result is false can be provided by extending the **if** statement with the **else** keyword.

An **else** statement follows after the **if** statement like this:

if (*condition* **)** *execute-this-statement-when-true* **;**

else *execute-this-statement-when-false* **;**

An **if-else** statement may also specify multiple statements to be executed by enclosing those statements within braces, like this:

```
if ( condition )
{
  execute-this-statement-when-true ;
  execute-this-statement-when-true ;
}
else
{
  execute-this-statement-when-false ;
  execute-this-statement-when-false ;
}
```

Multiple branches can be provided by making subsequent conditional **if** tests at the start of each **else** statement block like this:

```
if ( condition )
{
  execute-these-statements-when-true ;
}
else if ( condition )
{
  execute-these-statements-when-true ;
}
else if ( condition )
{
  execute-these-statements-when-true ;
}
else
{
  execute-these-statements-when-false ;
}
```

An **if-else-if** statement might repeatedly test a variable for a range of values or might test a variety of conditions. The final **else** statement acts as a default when no conditions are found to be true.

Hot tip

Once a condition is found to be true in an **if-else** statement its associated statements are executed, then flow continues after the **if-else** statement – without evaluating subsequent **else** statements.

1 Create an HTML document that embeds an external script file and contains an element in which to write

```
<script type = "text/javascript" src = "else.js" > </script>
<div id = "panel" > </div>
```

else.html

2 Create the JavaScript file with an "init" function to initialize a variable with the panel element object, a variable to store a boolean value, and a variable to store an integer

```
function init()
{
  var panel = document.getElementById( "panel" ) ;
  var flag = false ;
  var num = 10 ;
}
document.addEventListener( "DOMContentLoaded", init, false ) ;
```

else.js

3 Next, in the function block, test the boolean variable

```
if ( flag )
{  panel.innerHTML = "Power is On" ; }
else
{  panel.innerHTML = "Power is Off" ; }
```

4 Now, in the function block, test the integer variable

```
if ( num === 5 )
{  panel.innerHTML += "<br>Number is Five" ; }
else if ( num === 10 )
{
  panel.innerHTML += "<br>Number is Ten" ;
}
else
{ panel.innerHTML +=
                "<br>Number is Neither Five or Ten" ;
}
```

5 Save the script alongside the HTML document then open the page in a browser to see the result of each test

| ← → | 🗋 else.html | 🔎 → | ↑ ★ ☆ |

| 🗎 Else Conditional Test | ✕ |

Power is Off
Number is Ten

45

Hot tip

Notice how the variable storing the panel object can reference its properties and methods by appending them to the variable name – this is more efficient than repeatedly calling the document object's **getElementById()** method and makes the code more concise.

Switching alternatives

Conditionally branching script flow using **if-else** statements is fine for testing just a few conditions but can become unwieldy when there are a large number of conditions to test. In that situation it is often both more efficient and more elegant to use a **switch** statement rather than **if-else** statements.

A **switch** statement works in an unusual way – it first evaluates a specified expression, then seeks a match for the resulting value. Where a match is found, the **switch** statement will execute one or more statements associated with that value, otherwise it will execute one or more statements specified as "default statements".

The **switch** statement begins by enclosing the expression to be evaluated within parentheses after the **switch** keyword. This is followed by a pair of { } braces that contain the possible matches. Each match value follows a **case** keyword and employs a colon : character to associate one or more statements to be executed. Importantly, each **case** must end with a **break** statement to exit the **switch** statement after its associated statements have executed.

Optionally, a **switch** statement may include a final **default** alternative to associate one or more statements to be executed when none of the specified **case** values match the result of the expression evaluation.

So the syntax of a **switch** statement looks like this:

```
switch ( expression )
{
  case value-1 : statements-to-be-executed-when-matched ; break ;
  case value-2 : statements-to-be-executed-when-matched ; break ;
  case value-3 : statements-to-be-executed-when-matched ; break ;

  default : statements-to-be-executed-when-no-match-found ;
}
```

There is no limit to the number of **case** values that can be included within a **switch** statement block so this is an ideal way to match any one of tens, hundreds, or even thousands, of different values.

Beware

Omission of the break statement allows the script to also execute statements associated with subsequent unmatching case values.

46

1 Create an HTML document that embeds an external script file and contains an element in which to write

```
<script type = "text/javascript" src = "switch.js" >
</script> <div id = "panel" > </div>
```

switch.html

2 Create the JavaScript file with an "init" function to initialize a variable with the panel element object, and declare a variable in which to store a string value

```
function init()
{
  var panel = document.getElementById( "panel" ) ;
  var day ;
}
document.addEventListener( "DOMContentLoaded", init, false ) ;
```

switch.js

3 Next, in the function block, add a switch statement to assign a value to the string variable following an expression evaluation

```
switch ( 5 - 2 )
{
  case 1 : day = "Monday" ;        break ;
  case 2 : day = "Tuesday" ;       break ;
  case 3 : day = "Wednesday" ;   break ;
  case 4 : day = "Thursday" ;      break ;
  case 5 : day = "Friday" ;          break ;
  case 6 : day = "Saturday" ;      break ;
  case 7 : day = "Sunday" ;         break ;
  default : day = "There are only 7 days per week!" ;
}
```

4 Next, in the function block, after the switch statement, write the string into the panel

```
panel.innerHTML = "It's " + day ;
```

5 Save the script alongside the HTML document then open the page in a browser to see the assigned string value

Don't forget

String values offered as possible case matches must be enclosed within quotes like all other string values.

Looping for

A loop is a structure containing a test condition and one or more statements that are repeatedly executed while the test condition is met. Each single examination of the condition and execution of the statements is called an "iteration". When the test condition is not met no further iterations are made and flow continues at the next statement following the loop structure.

Probably the most commonly-used loop structure in JavaScript is the **for** loop, which has this syntax:

for (*initializer, condition, modifier*) { *statements-to-be-executed* }

The parentheses after the **for** keyword contain three expressions that control the number of iterations the loop will perform:

- Initializer – a statement that initializes a variable, which will be used to count the number of loop iterations, with a starting value. Traditionally this trivial counter variable is simply named "i".

- Condition – an expression that is tested for a boolean true value on each iteration. When the evaluation returns true, the loop statements are then executed to complete that iteration. If the evaluation returns false, the statements are not executed and the loop ends. Typically, the condition examines the value of the loop counter variable.

- Modifier – a statement that modifies a value in the test condition so that at some point its evaluation will return false. Typically this will increment, or decrement, the loop counter variable.

For example, a **for** loop structure to execute a set of statements one hundred times might look like this:

for (var i = 0 ; i < 100 ; i++) { *statements-to-be-executed* }

In this case the counter variable is incremented on each iteration until its value reaches 100, upon which the evaluation returns **false** and the loop ends.

1 Create an HTML document that embeds an external script file and contains an element in which to write

```
<script type = "text/javascript" src = "for.js" > </script>
<div id = "panel" > </div>
```

for.html

2 Create the JavaScript file with an "init" function to initialize a variable with the panel element object, and declare a variable in which to store a loop counter value

```
function init()
{
  var panel = document.getElementById( "panel" ) ;
  var i ;
}
document.addEventListener( "DOMContentLoaded", init, false ) ;
```

for.js

3 Next, in the function block, add a for loop structure to write a line containing the counter value into the panel on each iteration

```
for ( i = 1 ; i < 11 ; i++ )
{
  panel.innerHTML += "Iteration number: " + i + "<br>" ;
}
```

4 Save the script alongside the HTML document then open the page in a browser to see the lines written by the loop

```
For Loops

Iteration number: 1
Iteration number: 2
Iteration number: 3
Iteration number: 4
Iteration number: 5
Iteration number: 6
Iteration number: 7
Iteration number: 8
Iteration number: 9
Iteration number: 10
```

Don't forget

Optionally the braces may be omitted when the loop only executes a single statement, like the one listed here, but it is recommended you always include braces for code consistency.

Looping while true

The **for** loop structure, described in the previous example, is ideal when the number of required iterations is a known quantity but when this is unknown a **while** loop structure is often preferable:

```
while( condition )
{
  statements-to-be-executed ;
  modifier ;
}
```

The parentheses after the **while** keyword contain a condition that is evaluated for a boolean value upon each iteration. Statements to be executed on each iteration are enclosed within braces along with a statement that modifies a value in the test condition so that at some point its evaluation will return **false** and the loop will exit. While the evaluation remains **true** the statements will be executed on each iteration of the loop.

Where the condition evaluation is **false** on the first iteration, the loop exits immediately so the statements within its braces are never executed. Both **while** loops and **for** loops are sometimes referred to as "pre-test" loops because their test condition is evaluated before any statements are executed.

A **while** loop can be made to perform a specific number of iterations, like a **for** loop, by using a counter variable as the test condition and incrementing its value on each iteration. For example, a **while** loop structure to execute a set of statements one hundred times might look like this:

```
var i = 0 ;

while ( i < 100 )
{
  statements-to-be-executed ;
  i++ ;
}
```

The counter variable is incremented on each iteration until its value reaches 100, upon which the evaluation returns false and the loop ends.

1 Create an HTML document that embeds an external script file and contains an element in which to write
```
<script type = "text/javascript" src = "while.js" ></script>
<div id = "panel" > </div>
```

HTML

while.html

2 Create the JavaScript file with an "init" function to initialize a variable with the panel element object, and to initialize a variable with an integer value to be modified and tested by a loop
```
function init()
{
  var panel = document.getElementById( "panel" ) ;
  var num = 70 ;
}
document.addEventListener( "DOMContentLoaded", init, false ) ;
```

JS

while.js

3 Next, in the function block, add a while loop structure to write a line containing the current integer value into the panel, and to decrement its value by five on each iteration
```
while ( num > 10 )
{
  panel.innerHTML +=
            "Countdown value: " + num + "<br>" ;
  num -= 5 ;
}
```

4 Save the script alongside the HTML document then open the page in a browser to see the lines written by the loop

```
┌─────────────────────────────────────────────┐
│  while.html                      ⋔ ★ ☼        │
│  ⬅ ➡                                          │
│  ◎ While Loops            ✕                   │
│  Countdown value: 65                          │
│  Countdown value: 60                          │
│  Countdown value: 55                          │
│  Countdown value: 50                          │
│  Countdown value: 45                          │
│  Countdown value: 40                          │
│  Countdown value: 35                          │
│  Countdown value: 30                          │
│  Countdown value: 25                          │
│  Countdown value: 20                          │
│  Countdown value: 15                          │
│  Countdown value: 10                          │
└─────────────────────────────────────────────┘
```

Hot tip

Each while loop must have braces as they contain at least two statements – one statement to execute and a modifier.

Doing do-while loops

Another kind of loop available in JavaScript is the **do while** loop structure. This is like an inverted version of the **while** loop, described in the previous example, and is ideal when the statements it will execute on each iteration absolutely must be executed at least one time. Its syntax looks like this:

```
do
{
  statements-to-be-executed ;
  modifier ;
}
while ( condition ) ;
```

The parentheses after the **while** keyword contain a condition that is evaluated for a boolean value after each iteration. Statements to be executed on each iteration are enclosed within braces along with a statement that modifies a value in the test condition so that at some point its evaluation will return **false** and the loop will exit. While the evaluation remains **true** the statements will be executed on each iteration of the loop.

Where the condition evaluation is **false** on the first iteration the loop exits immediately so the statements within its braces have been executed once. The **do while** loop is sometimes referred to as a "post-test" loop because the test condition is evaluated after its statements have been executed.

A **do while** loop can be made to perform a specific number of iterations, like a **for** loop, by using a counter variable as the test condition and incrementing its value on each iteration.
For example, a **do while** loop structure to execute a set of statements one hundred times might look like this:

```
var i = 0 ;

do
{
  statements-to-be-executed ;
  i++ ;
}
while ( i < 100 ) ;
```

1 Create an HTML document that embeds an external script file and contains an element in which to write
```
<script type = "text/javascript" src = "dowhile.js">
</script><div id = "panel" > </div>
```

dowhile.html

2 Create the JavaScript file with an "init" function to initialize a variable with the panel element object, and to initialize a variable with an integer value to be modified and tested by a loop
```
function init()
{
  var panel = document.getElementById( "panel" ) ;
  var num = 2 ;
}
document.addEventListener( "DOMContentLoaded", init, false ) ;
```

dowhile.js

3 Next, in the function block, add a **do while** loop structure to write a line containing the current integer value into the panel, and to multiply its value by two on each iteration
```
do
{
  num *= 2 ;
  panel.innerHTML +=
              "Multiplied value: " + num + "<br>" ;
}
while ( num < 1000 ) ;
```

4 Save the script alongside the HTML document then open the page in a browser to see the lines written by the loop

```
dowhile.html
Do While Loops
Multiplied value: 4
Multiplied value: 8
Multiplied value: 16
Multiplied value: 32
Multiplied value: 64
Multiplied value: 128
Multiplied value: 256
Multiplied value: 512
Multiplied value: 1024
```

Don't forget

Notice that the final value exceeds the condition limit because it gets written before the test is made.

Breaking out of loops

The JavaScript **break** keyword can be used to exit from a loop when a specified condition is encountered. The conditional test should appear before all other statements to be executed so the loop will end immediately.

Where a **break** statement is used in a loop that is nested within an outer loop, flow resumes in the outer loop iteration. If it is desirable for the **break** statement to quit both inner and outer loops a label can be specified for the outer loop and in the **break** statement.

break.html

break.js

1. Create an HTML document that embeds an external script file and contains an element in which to write
```
<script type = "text/javascript" src = "break.js" >
</script> <div id = "panel" > </div>
```

2. Create the JavaScript file with an "init" function to initialize a variable with the panel element object, and to declare two variables to be used as loop iteration counters
```
function init()
{
  var panel = document.getElementById( "panel" ) ;
  var i , j ;
}
document.addEventListener( "DOMContentLoaded", init, false ) ;
```

3. Next in the function block, add a labeled loop containing an inner nested for loop with a "commented-out" break
```
quitLoop:
for ( i = 1 ; i < 4 ; i++ )
{
  panel.innerHTML += "<dt>Outer loop: " + i ;
  for ( j = 1 ; j < 4 ; j++ )
  {
    // if( j === 2 ) { break ; }
    panel.innerHTML += "<dd>Inner loop: " + j ;
  }
}
```

4. Save the script alongside the HTML document then open the page in a browser to see the lines written by the loops

Don't forget

The break keyword is also used as a terminator in switch statements.

5 Uncomment the break statement then save the JavaScript file and refresh the web page to see the inner loop quit
`if ( j === 2 ) { break ; }`

6 Edit the break statement to exit to the loop label then save the JavaScript file and refresh the web page to see both loops quit
`if ( j === 2 ) { break quitLoop ; }`

Beware

Don't be tempted to use break statements to exit loops in place of the regular conditional tests that form part of the loop structure.

Returning control

The JavaScript **continue** keyword can be used to exit from a single iteration of a loop when a specified condition is encountered. The conditional test should appear before all other statements to be executed, except a modifier, so the iteration will stop immediately and flow will resume at the start of the next iteration.

Multiple conditions can also be tested using the logical OR || operator to allow several specified iterations to be skipped.

continue.html

continue.js

Beware

Remember that the loop counter must be modified before any break or continue statements to avoid creating an infinite loop.

1. Create an HTML document that embeds an external script file and contains an element in which to write
```
<script type = "text/javascript" src = "continue.js" >
</script>
<div id = "panel" > </div>
```

2. Create the JavaScript file with an "init" function to initialize a variable with the panel element object, and to declare a variable that will be used as a loop counter
```
function init()
{
  var panel = document.getElementById( "panel" ) ;
  var i ;
}
document.addEventListener( "DOMContentLoaded", init, false ) ;
```

3. Next, in the function block, add a for loop to write ten lines in the panel
```
for ( i = 1 ; i < 11 ; i++ )
{
  // Continue statement may be added here.
  panel.innerHTML += "Loop iteration: " + i + "<br>" ;
}
```

4. Save the script alongside the HTML document then open the page in a browser to see the lines written by the loops

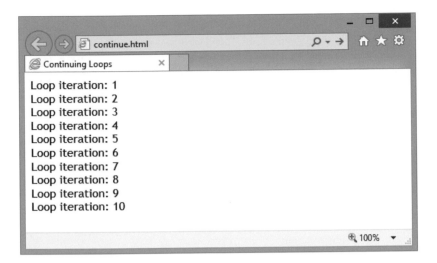

Hot tip

In statements containing multiple expressions it sometimes aids readability to enclose each expression within parentheses. For instance, with this example you may prefer ((i===2) || (i===7)).

5 Now, insert a continue statement to skip the second and seventh iterations of the loop at the start of the loop statements block

```
if ( i === 2 || i === 7 ) { continue ; }
```

6 Save the JavaScript file then refresh the web page to see the specified iterations are now omitted

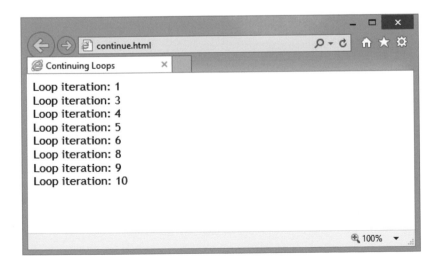

Summary

- An **if** statement performs a conditional test and will only execute the statements it contains when the evaluation is **true**

- An **else** statement can be added after an **if** statement to provide an alternative for when the evaluation is **false**

- Multiple alternative branches can be provided after an **if** statement with subsequent **else if** statements

- A **switch** statement is often preferable to an **if** statement when there are many conditions to test

- Each **case** statement must be terminated by a **break** keyword

- A **default** statement may be included at the end of a **switch** statement block to specify default statements to execute when no specified **case** values match the result of the evaluation

- The **for** loop begins with an initializer, a test condition, and a modifier within parentheses after the **for** keyword

- A loop modifier must change a value in the test condition so that the evaluation will become **false** and the loop will exit

- When the required number of iterations is an unknown quantity a **while** loop is often preferable to a **for** loop

- A **do while** loop can be used when the statements it contains absolutely must be executed at least once

- The statement block of a **while** loop and a **do while** loop must contain a modifier to change a value in the test condition

- A **break** statement immediately exits a loop

- Optionally, a loop structure may be labeled to allow a **break** statement in a nested loop to exit both loops

- A **continue** statement stops execution of a single iteration of a loop and flow resumes at the start of the next iteration

4 Employing objects

This chapter demonstrates how to create custom objects and how to use the built-in JavaScript Array object.

Creating an object

In JavaScript an "object" is a self-contained entity comprising of "properties" (variables) and "methods" (functions). An object can store data in its properties and perform tasks with its methods. There are three kinds of JavaScript object:

- **Built-in objects** – an intrinsic part of the JavaScript language with properties and methods that provide useful features, such as Date and Math functionality

- **DOM (Document Object Model) objects** – a hierarchical arrangement representing components of a web page beginning with the top-level window object

- **Custom objects** – author-specified to store data and provide functionality in a single entity

Understanding how to create and use custom objects makes it easy to understand built-in objects and DOM objects later. The custom object is defined by a prototype function that is a template specifying an object name, in accordance with the usual naming conventions, and properties and methods. The syntax of an object definition looks like this:

```
function object-name ( parameter1 , parameter2 , parameter3 )
{
  this.property1 = parameter1 ;
  this.property2 = parameter2 ;
  this.property3 = parameter3 ;

  this.method1 = function-name1 ;
  this.method2 = function-name2 ;
}
```

The object definition assigns the names of external functions to be its methods but its properties are initialized by values passed as arguments when an "instance" of the object is created (instantiated), using the **new** keyword. Each property or method can then be referenced by "dot syntax" – prefixing its name with the object name, such as *object.method*().

Don't forget

Object names may comprise letters, numbers, and underscore characters, but may not contain spaces or begin with a number. Additionally, you must avoid the JavaScript keywords and reserved words listed on page 11.

60

Hot tip

The **this** keyword, which is used to define the properties and methods in the object definition, means "belonging to this object".

1. Create an HTML document that embeds an external script file and contains an element in which to write
`<script type = "text/javascript" src = "object.js" > </script> <div id = "panel" > </div>`

object.html

2. Create the JavaScript file with an object definition containing three properties and one method
```
function Car( make , model , color )
{
  this.make = make ;
  this.model = model ;
  this.color = color ;
  this.accelerate = accelerate ;
}
```

object.js

3. Next, add the method function above the object definition
`function accelerate() { return "<br>Vroom!" ; }`

Don't forget

The name of the functions that define objects should begin with an uppercase character to differentiate them from regular functions.

4. Now, add an "init" function to initialize a variable with the panel element object, and to assign an instance of the custom object to a variable when the document loads
```
function init()
{
  var panel = document.getElementById( "panel" ) ;
  var myCar = new Car( "Dodge" , " Viper" , "Red " ) ;
}
document.addEventListener( "DOMContentLoaded", init, false ) ;
```

5. In the init function block, insert statements to write the object property values into the panel
```
panel.innerHTML = myCar.color+ myCar.make+ myCar.model ;
panel.innerHTML += myCar.accelerate() ;
```

Hot tip

Notice that **getElementById()** is a method of the DOM **document** object, and **onload** is a property of the DOM **window** object.

6. Save the script alongside the HTML document then open the page in a browser to see the object properties

61

Extending an object

Custom objects are very flexible and can easily be extended using an intrinsic **prototype** property to add more object properties or methods, with *object-name.**prototype**.property/method-name*.

Both original and extended object property values can be changed at any time simply by assigning a new value, using dot syntax to reference the property as *object-name.property-name*.

A special **for in** loop can be used to list all the initialized properties and methods of an object with this syntax:

```
for ( property in object-name )
{
        if ( property !== "" ) { statements-to-execute }
}
```

In order to reference the value of each property on each iteration the property name should be enclosed within square brackets following the object name as *object-name*[property].

prototype.html

prototype.js

1. Create an HTML document that embeds an external script file and contains an element in which to write
```
<script type = "text/javascript" src = "prototype.js" >
</script> <div id = "panel" > </div>
```

2. Create the JavaScript file with an object definition containing just three properties
```
function Car( make , model , color )
{
  this.make = make ;
  this.model = model ;
  this.color = color ;
}
```

3. Now, add an "init" function to initialize a variable with the panel element object, and to assign an instance of the custom object
```
function init()
{
  var panel = document.getElementById( "panel" ) ;
  var myCar = new Car( "Ford" , " Focus" , "Blue" ) ;
}
document.addEventListener( "DOMContentLoaded", init, false ) ;
```

4   Next, in the init function block, insert a statement
to extend the object by adding another property and
assigning it a value
Car.prototype.doors = 4 ;

5   Next, insert a loop to write the name and value of each
object property in the panel, and a final ruled line
```
for ( property in myCar )
{
  if ( myCar[ property ] !== "" )
  {   panel.innerHTML +=
        ( property + ": " + myCar[ property ] + "<br>" ) ;
  }
}
panel.innerHTML += "<hr>" ;
```

6   Now, insert statements assigning new values to each property
myCar.make = "Dodge" ;
myCar.model = "Challenger" ;
myCar.color = "Orange" ;
myCar.doors = 2 ;

7   Repeat the loop listed in step 5 – this time to write the
name and new value of each object property in the panel

8   Save the script alongside the HTML document then open
the page in a browser to see the object properties and values

Creating an array object

An array is a JavaScript built-in object that can store multiple items of various data-types in individual "elements". An array instance is traditionally created using the JavaScript **new** keyword, the **Array()** object constructor, and a variable name assignment. Additionally the statement may also pass values to initialize array elements. For example, to create a new array named "colors":

var colors = new Array(*value1* , *value2* , *value3*) ;

An alternative, more succinct, way to create an array is to simply assign the initial element value list within a pair of square brackets – these imply that the values are to be stored in elements so an array literal gets created:

var colors = [*value1* , *value2* , *value3*] ;

Array literals are supported by all modern browsers so the creation of arrays with this more succinct syntax is now recommended. Should there be a need for a script to be backward-compatible with really old browsers the **Array()** constructor can be used instead.

Unlike custom objects, where each property is named, array elements are automatically numbered – starting at zero. So the first element is 0, the second is 1, the third is 2, and so on. This numbering system is often referred to as a "zero-based index".

The value stored within an array element can be referenced by enclosing its element index number within square brackets following the object name. For example, **colors[0]** would reference the value in the first element in an array named "colors".

Where array elements are not required to be initialized immediately an empty array can be created and values assigned to its elements later, like this:

var colors = [] ;   // Equivalent to assigning a new Array() ;

colors[0] = "Red" ;

colors[1] = "White" ;

colors[2] = "Blue" ;

Don't forget

All built-in object names begin with an uppercase character – so the constructor is named "Array", not "array".

1 Create an HTML document that embeds an external script file and contains an element in which to write
```
<script type = "text/javascript" src = "array.js" >
</script> <div id = "panel" > </div>
```

array.html

2 Create the JavaScript file with an "init" function to initialize a variable with the panel element object
```
function init()
{
  var panel = document.getElementById( "panel" ) ;
}
document.addEventListener( "DOMContentLoaded", init, false ) ;
```

array.js

3 In the function block, insert a statement to create an array initialized with a different month name in each element
```
var summer = [ "June" , "July" , "August" ] ;
```

4 Next, in the function block, insert a loop to write the index number and value of each array element into the panel
```
for ( month in summer )
{
  if ( summer[ month ] !== "" )
  { panel.innerHTML +=
       ( month + ": " + summer[ month ] + "<br>" ) ; }
}
```

5 Now, insert a statement to write one selected array element into the panel
```
panel.innerHTML += "Vacation month: " + summer[2] ;
```

6 Save the script alongside the HTML document then open the page in a browser to see the array element numbers and values

---

array.html 🔍 Array Objects ✕

```
0: June
1: July
2: August
Vacation month: August
```

65

Looping through elements

Arrays and loops make great partners! Any kind of loop can be used to fill the elements of an array with values. The elements of even very large arrays can be "populated" in this way – and with surprisingly little code.

Similarly, loops can be used to quickly read the values in each array element and perform some action appropriate to that value on each iteration of the loop.

Usefully, each array has a **length** property that contains an integer record of the total number of elements in that array. As a result of zero-based indexing this will always be one greater than the final element's index number so can be used in a conditional test to terminate the loop.

elements.html

elements.js

① Create an HTML document that embeds an external script file and contains an element in which to write
<script type = "text/javascript" src = "elements.js" > </script> <div id = "panel" > </div>

② Create the JavaScript file with an "init" function to initialize a variable with the panel element object, and to declare a counter variable and an empty array
```
function init()
{
  var panel = document.getElementById( "panel" ) ;
  var i , arr = [] ;
}
document.addEventListener( "DOMContentLoaded", init, false ) ;
```

③ Next, in the function block, insert a loop to fill ten elements with a boolean value, according to the parity of their index number, and write their index number and value in the panel
```
panel.innerHTML = "Fill Elements..." ;

for ( i = 1 ; i < 11 ; i++ )
{
  arr[ i ] = ( i % 2 === 0 ) ? true : false ;
  panel.innerHTML += "<br>Element " + i + " : " + arr[ i ] ;
}
```

4 Now, in the function block, insert a loop to read each element and write the index number of true elements in the panel

```
panel.innerHTML += "<hr>Read Elements...<br>True: " ;
for ( i = 1 ; i < arr.length ; i++ )
{
  if ( arr[ i ] ) { panel.innerHTML += i + " " ; }
}
```

5 Finally, in the function block, insert a loop to read each element and write the index number of false elements into the panel

```
panel.innerHTML += "<br>False: " ;
for ( i = 1 ; i < arr.length ; i++ )
{
  if ( !arr[ i ] ) { panel.innerHTML += i + " " ; }
}
```

6 Save the script alongside the HTML document then open the page in your browser to see the array elements filled and read

Hot tip

This array length property has a value of 11 because the array has 11 elements – even though element zero has not been filled.

---

elements.html

Loops and Array Elements ✕

Fill Elements...
Element 1 : false
Element 2 : true
Element 3 : false
Element 4 : true
Element 5 : false
Element 6 : true
Element 7 : false
Element 8 : true
Element 9 : false
Element 10 : true

Read Elements...
True: 2 4 6 8 10
False: 1 3 5 7 9

100%

Don't forget

Conditional tests for a boolean value do not need to include the expression === true as that is automatic.

Adding array elements

The array **length** property, that was used in the previous example to terminate a loop, after reading the final element in an array, can be used to resize an array by adding or subtracting elements. Simple statements can increase an array using the + addition operator or reduce an array with the – subtraction operator.

Additionally, the array **length** property can be used in the body of a loop structure to dynamically add an element on each iteration of the loop. As the **length** value is always one greater than the index number of the final element it can be used to reference the next element index value. For example **arr[arr.length]** references the next element beyond the current final element. Assigning the next element a value increases the array by one element so that on each further iteration the **length** property is incremented by one.

The values contained in all elements of an array can be returned as a comma-separated list just by using the array name in a statement.

resize.html

resize.js

1 Create an HTML document that embeds an external script file and contains an element in which to write
<script type = "text/javascript" src = "resize.js" >
</script> <div id = "panel" > </div>

2 Create the JavaScript file with an "init" function to initialize a variable with the panel element object, and to declare a counter variable when the document has loaded
function init()
{
  var panel = document.getElementById("panel") ;
  var i ;
}
document.addEventListener("DOMContentLoaded", init, false) ;

3 Next, in the function block, create and initialize two arrays
var week = ["Mon" , "Tue" , "Wed" , "Thu" , "Fri"] ;
var weekend = ["Sat" , "Sun"] ;

4 Now, in the function block, write the value of all the elements of each array in the panel
panel.innerHTML = "Weekdays: " + week ;
panel.innerHTML += "<hr>Weekend days: " + weekend ;

5 In the function block, insert a loop to add an element to the first array on each iteration – assigning values from each element of the second array

```
for ( i = 0 ; i < weekend.length ; i ++ )
{
  week[ week.length ] = weekend[ i ] ;
}
```

6 Next, in the function block, write the value of all elements of the increased array in the panel

```
panel.innerHTML +=
        "<hr>Increased with weekend days: " + week ;
```

7 Now, in the function block, reduce the size of the extended array

```
week.length -= 2 ;
```

8 Finally, in the function block, write the value of all elements of the reduced array in the panel

```
panel.innerHTML +=
        "<hr>Reduced back to weekdays: " + week ;
```

9 Save the script alongside the HTML document then open the page in a browser to see the element values as the array is resized

Beware

Setting an array's length to zero will remove all elements and lose their values.

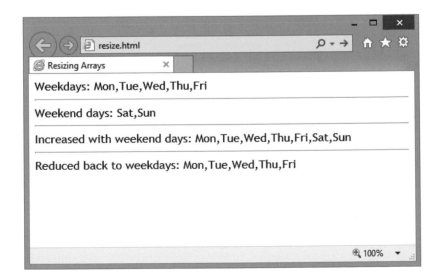

Hot tip

Notice that when the length property is reduced elements are removed from the end of the array, not from its beginning.

69

Joining and slicing arrays

JavaScript objects have properties and methods. In addition to the length property, each array object has methods that can be used to manipulate the elements in an array. These are listed in the table below together with a brief description of the task they perform:

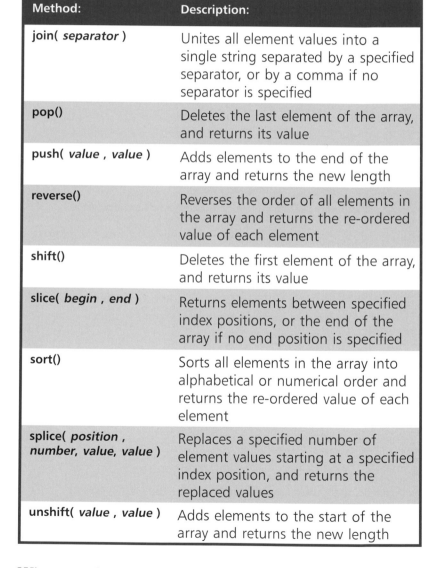

Method:	Description:
join(*separator* **)**	Unites all element values into a single string separated by a specified separator, or by a comma if no separator is specified
pop()	Deletes the last element of the array, and returns its value
push(*value* , *value* **)**	Adds elements to the end of the array and returns the new length
reverse()	Reverses the order of all elements in the array and returns the re-ordered value of each element
shift()	Deletes the first element of the array, and returns its value
slice(*begin* , *end* **)**	Returns elements between specified index positions, or the end of the array if no end position is specified
sort()	Sorts all elements in the array into alphabetical or numerical order and returns the re-ordered value of each element
splice(*position* , *number, value, value* **)**	Replaces a specified number of element values starting at a specified index position, and returns the replaced values
unshift(*value* , *value* **)**	Adds elements to the start of the array and returns the new length

Where no values are specified by the **push()** or **unshift()** methods a single empty element gets added to the array. A comma-separated list of values can be specified to the **push()**, **unshift()**, and **splice()** methods to change multiple elements.

1 Create an HTML document that embeds an external script file and contains an element in which to write

```
<script type = "text/javascript" src = "slice.js" > </script>
<div id = "panel" > </div>
```

slice.html

2 Create the JavaScript file with an "init" function to initialize a variable with the panel element object, and to initialize an array

```
function init()
{
  var panel = document.getElementById( "panel" ) ;
  var seasons = [ "Spring" , "Summer" , "Fall" , "Winter" ] ;
}
document.addEventListener( "DOMContentLoaded", init, false ) ;
```

slice.js

3 In the function block, insert statements to manipulate the array elements and write the result of each task in the panel

```
panel.innerHTML = "Elements: " + seasons ;
panel.innerHTML += "<br>Joined: " + seasons.join( " and" ) ;
panel.innerHTML += "<hr>Popped: " + seasons.pop() ;
panel.innerHTML += "<br>Elements: " + seasons ;
panel.innerHTML +="<hr>Pushed: "+seasons.push("Winter");
panel.innerHTML += "<br>Elements: " + seasons ;
panel.innerHTML += "<hr>Sliced: " + seasons.slice( 1 , 3 ) ;
panel.innerHTML +=
        "<br>Spliced: " + seasons.splice( 2 , 1 , "Autumn") ;
panel.innerHTML += "<br>Elements: " + seasons ;
```

Hot tip

Use the **slice()** method without a replacement value to delete a specified number of elements at a specified position and it will automatically renumber all remaining elements that follow in that array.

71

4 Save the script alongside the HTML document then open the page in a browser to see the changing array elements

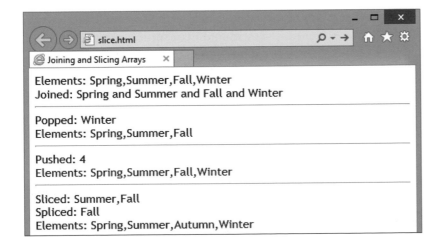

slice.html

Joining and Slicing Arrays

Elements: Spring,Summer,Fall,Winter
Joined: Spring and Summer and Fall and Winter

Popped: Winter
Elements: Spring,Summer,Fall

Pushed: 4
Elements: Spring,Summer,Fall,Winter

Sliced: Summer,Fall
Spliced: Fall
Elements: Spring,Summer,Autumn,Winter

Don't forget

The **shift()** and **unshift()** methods work like **pop()** and **push()** but on the first element rather than the last. The **reverse()** and **sort()** methods are used in the next example listed overleaf.

Sorting array elements

It is often desirable to arrange an array's element values in a particular order using the array **sort()** method. This can optionally specify a comparison function argument to define the sort order.

When no comparison function is specified the **sort()** method will, by default, convert all element values to strings then sort them lexicographically in dictionary order – comparing each first character, then each second character, and so on. Where the elements contain matching strings that differ only by character case the string with most uppercase characters gets a lower index position – appearing before that with fewer uppercase characters.

The **sort()** method's default behavior of sorting into dictionary order is usually satisfactory for string values but is often not what you want when sorting numerical values. For example, in sorting three values 30, 100, 20 the result is 100, 20, 30 – because the first characters are different they are sorted by that comparison only. Typically it is preferable to require all numerical element values to be sorted in ascending, or descending, numerical order so the **sort()** method needs to specify the name of a custom comparison function to define the sort order.

A comparison function nominated by the **sort()** method will be passed successive pairs of element values for comparison and it must return an integer value to indicate each comparison's result. When the first value is greater than the second it should return a value greater than zero to indicate that the first value should be sorted to a higher index position – to appear after the second value. Conversely, the comparison function should return a value less than zero to indicate that the first value should be sorted to a lower index position – to appear before the second value. When both values are identical zero should be returned to indicate that the element positions should remain unchanged. When all comparisons have been made the elements will be arranged in ascending value order. If descending order is required the array's **reverse()** method can then be used to reverse the element order.

If a comparison function is comparing numerical element values it simply needs to return the result of subtracting the second passed value from the first passed value to have the desired effect.

① Create an HTML document that embeds an external script file and contains an element in which to write

```
<script type = "text/javascript" src = "sort.js" > </script>
<div id = "panel" > </div>
```

sort.html

② Create the JavaScript file with an "init" function to initialize a variable with the panel element object, and to initialize two arrays

```
function init()
{
  var panel = document.getElementById( "panel" ) ;
  var hues = [ "Red" , "RED" , "red" , "Green" , "Blue" ] ;
  var nums = [ 1 , 20 , 3 , 45 , 44 , 0.5 ] ;
}
document.addEventListener( "DOMContentLoaded", init, false ) ;
```

sort.js

③ In the function block, insert statements to manipulate the array elements and write the result of each task in the panel

```
panel.innerHTML = "Colors: " + hues ;
panel.innerHTML +="<br>Dictionary sort: " + hues.sort() ;
panel.innerHTML += "<hr>Numbers: " + nums ;
panel.innerHTML +="<br>Dictionary sort: "+ nums.sort() ;
panel.innerHTML +=
        "<br>Numerical sort: " + nums.sort( sortNums ) ;
panel.innerHTML += "<br>Reversed: " + nums.reverse() ;
```

73

④ Above the init function, add a custom comparison function to sort numerically in ascending order

```
function sortNums( x , y ) { return ( x - y ) ; }
```

Beware

⑤ Save the script alongside the HTML document then open the page in a browser to see the sorted array elements

When the **sort()** method specifies a comparison function it must nominate it by function name only – do not include trailing brackets after the comparison function name in the argument to the **sort()** method.

```
 ⬅ ➡  🔲 sort.html                          🔍 ▾ →   🏠 ★ ☼
 🌐 Sorting Array Elements       ✕

 Colors: Red,RED,red,Green,Blue
 Dictionary sort: Blue,Green,RED,Red,red
 ────────────────────────────────────────────
 Numbers: 1,20,3,45,44,0.5
 Dictionary sort: 0.5,1,20,3,44,45
 Numerical sort: 0.5,1,3,20,44,45
 Reversed: 45,44,20,3,1,0.5
```

Catching exceptions

Sections of script in which it is possible to anticipate errors, such as those handling user input, may be enclosed in a **try catch** structure to handle "exception" errors. The statements to be executed are contained within the braces of a **try** block and exceptions are passed as an argument to the ensuing **catch** block for handling. Optionally, this may be followed by a **finally** block, containing statements to execute after exceptions have been handled.

JavaScript recognizes error objects named **Error**, **RangeError**, **EvalError**, **TypeError**, **SyntaxError**, and **URIError**. These may be automatically created and passed to the catch block by the parser or manually created with the new keyword and a constructor, then passed using the **throw** keyword.

Each error object can have a **name** property and a **message** property to allow the **catch** block to describe its nature. The message is specified as an argument to the constructor for error objects created manually, but is predefined otherwise.

Alternatively, a string may be passed to the **catch** block by the **throw** keyword to identify the error. An appropriate action can then be determined by examining the string value and multiple alternatives can be provided by a **switch** statement.

trycatch.html

trycatch.js

1 Create an HTML document that embeds an external script file and contains an element in which to write
```
<script type = "text/javascript" src = "trycatch.js" >
</script>
<div id = "panel" > </div>
```

2 Create the JavaScript file with an "init" function to initialize a variable with the panel element object, and to declare and initialize a variable whose value may cause exceptions
```
function init()
{
  var panel = document.getElementById( "panel" ) ;
  var day = 32 ;
}
document.addEventListener( "DOMContentLoaded", init, false ) ;
```

3 Next, in the function block, insert a try catch finally statement

```
try
{
  if ( day > 31 )
  { throw new RangeError( " 'day' cannot exceed 31" ) ; }
  if ( day <  1 ) { throw "GetReal" ; }
}
catch( err )
{
  panel.innerHTML= ( err === "GetReal" ) ?
("Ooops! The 'day' variable has an invalid value of "+day ) :
( err.name + " exception has occurred: " + err.message ) ;
}
finally
{
  panel.innerHTML += "<br>The script has ignored that
                      variable and is continuing..." ;
}
```

Beware

Enclosing statements within **try catch** structures provides a great way to catch errors but it incurs a performance penalty. Only use **try catch** statements where they are absolutely needed.

4 Save the script alongside the HTML document then open the web page in a browser to see a **RangeError** exception

Hot tip

Delete or comment-out the day variable declaration then save and refresh this example to see an automatic **TypeError** get caught.

5 Edit the variable assignment, changing its value to zero, then save the amended script and refresh the browser to see the new exception caught by the custom error handler

```
var day = 0 ;
```

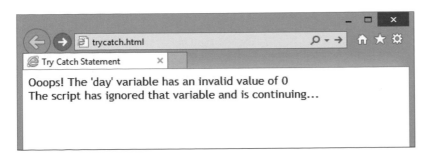

Summary

- An object is a self-contained entity comprising properties that store data and methods that perform tasks

- JavaScript has three types of object – built-in objects, DOM objects, and custom objects

- A custom object is defined by a prototype function that specifies the object name, properties, and methods

- Properties can be initialized by parameters passed when an instance of the custom is created using the **new** keyword

- Custom objects can be extended using their intrinsic **prototype** property to add properties or methods

- Instances of a custom object inherit all properties and methods of the prototype, including extended ones

- An array is a JavaScript built-in object that can store multiple items of data in individual elements

- The **new** keyword and the **Array()** constructor can be used to create an array instance for assignment to a named variable

- Array elements are automatically numbered from zero and each array element can be referenced by stating its index number within square brackets after the array variable name

- Loops are a great way to populate the elements of an array or to read each element's value on successive iterations

- Arrays have a **length** property that can be used to terminate a loop or to resize the array

- By default, the **sort()** method of an array object converts all element values to strings, then sorts them in dictionary order, unless a comparison function is specified as its argument

- Exception errors can be thrown from a try block to a catch block for error-handling and their name and message properties can describe the nature of the error

5 Telling the time

This chapter demonstrates how to use the built-in JavaScript date object to perform date and time tasks.

Getting the date

The built-in JavaScript Date object provides components representing a particular date, time, and timezone. An instance of a Date object is created using the **new** keyword, a **Date()** object constructor, and a variable name assignment. Without specifying any arguments to the constructor, a new Date object represents the date and time of its creation based upon the system time of the computer on which the browser is running. There is no consideration given as to whether system time is accurate to the Universal Time Clock (UTC) or Greenwich Mean Time (GMT).

Computer date and time is measured numerically as the period of elapsed time since January 1, 1970 00:00:00 – a point in time often referred to as the "epoch". In JavaScript the elapsed time is recorded as the number of milliseconds since the epoch. This figure can be extracted from Date object using its **getTime()** method and may be subtracted from that of another Date object to calculate an elapsed period between two points in a script. For example to calculate the period taken to execute a loop.

A string of the components within a Date object can be extracted using its **toString()** method, or an equivalent converted to UTC time using its **toUTCString()** method.

JavaScript can determine in which time zone the user is located, assuming the system is correctly set to the local time zone, by examining the value returned by a current Date object's **getTimezoneOffset()** method. This returns an integer value that is the number of minutes by which the current local time differs from UTC time. The calculation is performed in minutes rather than hours because some time zones are offset by other than one-hour intervals. For example, Newfoundland, Canada is UTC -3:30 (UTC -2:30 during periods of daylight saving time).

The time zone offset value can be used to provide localized customization for U.S. time zones but they must be adjusted by subtracting 60 (minutes) for periods of daylight saving time. The example opposite passes the current system date to a function that compares it against DST start and finish dates for that year then returns zero or 60 to adjust the time zone offset value accordingly.

Beware

The system time information can be easily changed by the user to any time, date, or time zone, so may not necessarily report their actual location.

1 Create an HTML document that embeds an external script file and contains an element in which to write
```
<script type = "text/javascript" src = "date.js" > </script>
<div id = "panel" > </div>
```

date.html

2 Create the JavaScript file with an "init" function to initialize four variables
```
function init()
{
  var panel = document.getElementById( "panel" ) ;
  var now = new Date() ;
  var offset = now.getTimezoneOffset() ;
  var dst = isDst( now ) ; // Call a function to adjust offset.
}
document.addEventListener( "DOMContentLoaded", init, false ) ;
```

date.js

3 Next, in the function block, insert a switch statement to match the adjusted time zone offset value
```
switch ( offset )
{
  case ( 300 - dst ) : offset = "East Coast" ; break ;
  case ( 360 - dst ) : offset = "Central" ; break ;
  case ( 420 - dst ) : offset = "Mountain" ; break ;
  case ( 480 - dst ) : offset = "Pacific" ; break ;
  default : offset = "all" ;
}
```

4 Now, in the function block, insert statements to write local and UTC date strings and a localized time zone greeting
```
panel.innerHTML = "System Time: " + now.toString() ;
panel.innerHTML +=
        "<br>UTC (GMT) Time: " + now.toUTCString() +
        "<hr>Welcome to " + offset + " visitors" ;
```

5 Save the script alongside the HTML document then open the page in a browser to see dates and local message

System Time: Tue Oct 8 03:18:16 EDT 2013
UTC (GMT) Time: Tue, 8 Oct 2013 07:18:16 UTC

Welcome to East Coast visitors

Hot tip

Discovery of the user's local time zone could be used to direct the browser to a page relevant to that time zone. For example, a page containing only Californian distributors for users in the Pacific time zone.

Extracting date components

A JavaScript Date object provides separate methods to extract each of its date components for the year, month name, day of the month, and the day name.

The Date object's **getFullYear()** method returns the year as a full four digit number, such as 2013, and the Date object's **getDate()** method returns the day number of the month – so that on the first day of the month it returns 1.

For reasons of internationalization **getMonth()** and **getDay()** return index number values that must be converted to the local language month and day names by the script. The conversion is easily made for month names by creating an array of all month names, starting with January, then using the index number returned by **getMonth()** to reference the appropriate month name. Similarly, the conversion is made for day names by creating an array of all day names, starting with Sunday, then using the index number returned by **getDay()** to reference the appropriate day name.

The various components can then be assembled into a date string arranged according to the preferred date format of any locale.

Beware

There is also a **getYear()** method which returns the full year in Internet Explorer but a value from the 1900 baseline year on Mozilla browsers, such as Firefox. So for 2013 it returns 113. Always use the **getFullYear()** method instead of **getYear()**.

months.html

months.js

1. Create an HTML document that embeds an external script file and contains an element in which to write
```
<script type = "text/javascript" src = "months.js" >
</script> <div id = "panel" > </div>
```

2. Create the JavaScript file with an "init" function to initialize three variables
```
function init()
{
  var panel = document.getElementById( "panel" ) ;

  var days =
[ "Sun" , "Mon" , "Tue" , "Wed" , "Thu" , "Fri" , "Sat" ] ;

  var months = [ "Jan" , "Feb" , "Mar" , "Apr" , "May" ,
"Jun" , "Jul" , "Aug" , "Sep" , "Oct" , "Nov" , "Dec" ] ;

}
document.addEventListener( "DOMContentLoaded", init, false ) ;
```

3 Next, in the function block, create a new instance of the Date object
```
var now = new Date() ;
```

4 Now, in the function block, insert statements to extract date components using methods of the Date instance
```
var yy = now.getFullYear() ;    // Year.
var mm = now.getMonth() ;    // Month name index.
var dd = now.getDate() ;  // Day of the month number.
var dy = now.getDay() ;       // Day name index.
```

5 Insert statements in the function block to convert extracted index numbers to month and day name values
```
mm = months[ mm ] ;  // Convert to month name string.
dy = days[ dy ] ;       // Convert to day name string.
```

6 Finally, in the function block, write date strings in the panel – in both American and European date formats
```
var str = dy + ", " + mm + " " + dd + ", " + yy ;
panel.innerHTML += "US Date String: " + str ;
str = dy + ", " + dd + " " + mm + ", " + yy ;
panel.innerHTML += "<br>UK Date String: " + str ;
```

7 Save the script alongside the HTML document then open the page in your browser to see the date strings

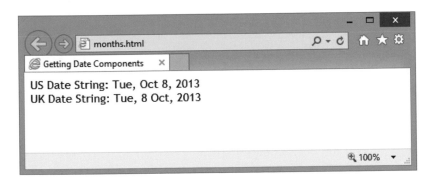

```
months.html
Getting Date Components
US Date String: Tue, Oct 8, 2013
UK Date String: Tue, 8 Oct, 2013

100%
```

Don't forget

Month indexing starts at zero, not one – so for example March is at index [2] not at [3].

Extracting time components

Just as a JavaScript Date object provides separate methods to extract each of its date components it also provides separate methods to extract each of its time components.

The Date object's **getHours()** method returns the hour in 24-hour format – as a value in the range 0-23. The **getMinutes()** and **getSeconds()** methods both return a value in the range 0-59. There is also a **getMilliseconds()** method for even greater precision that returns a value in the range 0-999.

The values of each component can be concatenated into a time string but it is often preferable to add a leading zero to single minute and second values for better readability. For example, 10:05:02 is preferable to 10:5:2.

An appropriate greeting string can be created by examining the hour value to establish whether the user's system time is currently morning, afternoon, or evening.

For situations where a 12-hour time format is desirable an "AM" or "PM" suffix can be created by examining the hour value and all PM hour values reduced by twelve. For example 13:00 can be transformed to 1:00 PM.

Don't forget

Time components are based upon the user's system time – which may not be accurate.

minutes.html

minutes.js

1. Create an HTML document that embeds an external script file and contains an element in which to write
```
<script type = "text/javascript" src = "minutes.js" >
</script> <div id = "panel" > </div>
```

2. Create the JavaScript file with an "init" function to initialize six variables
```
function init()
{
  var panel = document.getElementById( "panel" ) ;
  var now = new Date() ;
  var hh = now.getHours() ;
  var mn = now.getMinutes() ;
  var ss = now.getSeconds() ;
  var ms = now.getMilliseconds() ;
}
document.addEventListener( "DOMContentLoaded", init, false ) ;
```

3 Next, in the function block, insert statements to add leading zeros to single minutes and seconds values
```
if ( mn < 10 ) { mn = "0" + mn ; }
if ( ss < 10 ) { ss = "0" + ss ; }
```

4 Now, in the function block, create a time string and write it in the panel
```
var tim = hh + ":" + mn + ":" + ss + ":" +
                        " and " + ms + " milliseconds" ;
panel.innerHTML += "It's now: " + tim ;
```

5 Insert statements in the function block to create a greeting appropriate to the hour and write it in the panel
```
var hi = "Good Morning." ;                  // 0-11
if ( hh > 11 ) { hi = "Good Afternoon." ; }  // 12-17
if ( hh > 17 ) { hi = "Good Evening." ; }    // 18-23
panel.innerHTML += "<br>" + hi ;
```

6 Finally, in the function block, create a suffix appropriate to the hour and convert hour values to 12-hour format, then write the transformed date string in the panel
```
var suffix = ( hh > 11 ) ? " P.M." : " A.M." ;
if ( hh > 12 ) { hh -= 12 ; }
panel.innerHTML +=
        "<br>Time is: " + hh + ":" + mn + suffix ;
```

7 Save the script alongside the HTML document then open the page in your browser to see the time strings

> ### Hot tip
>
> The **Date** object also provides methods to retrieve the UTC equivalent of each date and time component. For example, **getUTCMonth()**, and **getUTCHours()**.

Setting the date and time

The JavaScript **Date()** constructor can optionally specify two to seven arguments to set values for each of its components like this:

new Date(*year, month, date, hours, minutes, seconds, milliseconds* **);**

When only the minimum year and month values are set, the date gets set to one and all time components are set to zero.

The Date object also provides separate methods to set the value of each of its date and time components individually. An argument to the **setFullYear()** method sets the year as a four-digit number and an argument to its **setMonth()** method sets the month numerically in the range 0-11 (0=January, 11=December). The **setDate()** method sets the day of the month number component, the **setHours()** method sets the hour component in the range 0-23, and the **setMinutes()** and **setSeconds()** methods set their respective components by each accepting an argument in the range 0-59. There is also a **setMilliseconds()** method to set the milliseconds component in the range 0-999.

The values of each set component can be revealed by displaying the entire Date object. Additionally, all Date objects have methods to output a variety of strings displaying date and time. The **toString()** method converts the date to a string value, the **toUTCString()** method converts the date to its UTC equivalent, and the **toLocaleString()** method displays the date using the computer's locale conventions. Useful **toDateString()** and **toTimeString()** methods can be used to display the date and time components.

setdate.html

setdate.js

1 Create an HTML document that embeds an external script file and contains an element in which to write
<script type = "text/javascript" src = "setdate.js" > </script> <div id = "panel" > </div>

2 Create the JavaScript file with an "init" function to initialize a variable, when the document has loaded
function init()
{
  var panel = document.getElementById("panel") ;
}
document.addEventListener("DOMContentLoaded", init, false) ;

3 Next, in the function block, insert statements to create a Date object and displays its components

```
var hol = new Date( 2014 , 6 , 4 ) ;
panel.innerHTML = "Object: " + hol ;
```

4 Now, in the function block, insert statements to individually set each component of the Date object to a new value

```
hol.setFullYear( 2013 ) ;
hol.setMonth( 11 ) ;
hol.setDate( 25 ) ;
hol.setHours( 12 ) ;
hol.setMinutes( 0 ) ;
hol.setSeconds( 0 ) ;
hol.setMilliseconds( 0 ) ;
```

5 Finally, in the function block, add statements to write various strings of the Date object's values in the panel

```
panel.innerHTML += "<br>String: " + hol.toString() ;
panel.innerHTML += "<br>UTC: " + hol.toUTCString() ;
panel.innerHTML += "<br>Locale: " + hol.toLocaleString() ;
panel.innerHTML += "<br>Date: " + hol.toDateString() ;
panel.innerHTML += "<br>Time: " + hol.toTimeString() ;
```

6 Save the script alongside the HTML document then open the page in your browser to see the date and time strings

Hot tip

The Date object also has a **setTime()** method that accepts an argument of the number of milliseconds since the epoch – each day has 86,400,000 milliseconds, so **setTime(86400000)** sets the date Jan 1,1970.

```
setdate.html                                    🔍 ▾ →   ⌂ ★ ✿
Setting the Date and Time     ✕

Object: Fri Jul 4 00:00:00 UTC+0300 2014
String: Wed Dec 25 12:00:00 UTC+0200 2013
UTC: Wed, 25 Dec 2013 10:00:00 UTC
Locale: Wednesday, December 25, 2013 12:00:00 PM
Date: Wed Dec 25 2013
Time: 12:00:00 UTC+0200

                                              🔍 100%  ▾
```

Summary

- JavaScript has a built-in Date object to represent date, time, and timezone components of a particular point in time

- A Date object is created using the **new** keyword and the **Date()** constructor

- Where no arguments are specified to the **Date()** constructor a Date object is created based upon the system time clock

- JavaScript Date objects record the elapsed number of milliseconds since the epoch at January 1, 1970 00:00:00 and its value can be found using the object's **getTime()** method

- The components of a Date object can be converted to a string value with its **toString()** or **toUTCString()** methods

- A Date object's **getTimezoneOffset()** method returns the number of minutes that local time differs from UTC time

- Individual Date components can be retrieved using **getFullYear()**, **getMonth()**, **getDate()**, and **getDay()** methods

- Individual time components can be retrieved from a Date object using its **getHours()**, **getMinutes()**, **getSeconds()**, and **getMilliseconds()** methods

- The **Date()** constructor can optionally accept up to seven arguments to set each of the date and time components

- Individual date and time components can be set for a Date object using its **setFullYear()**, **setMonth()**, **setDate()**, **setHours()**, **setMinutes()**, **setSeconds()**, and **setMilliseconds()** methods

- The **toLocaleString()** method returns a string using the computer's locale conventions while **toDateString()** and **toTimeString()** methods display the date and time components

6

Working with numbers and strings

This chapter demonstrates how to use the built-in Math and String objects, and internal methods.

Calculating circle values

JavaScript has a built-in Math object that provides a number of useful methods and constant mathematical values. The constants are listed in the table below together with their approximate value:

Hot tip

All the Math methods are listed on page 90.

Constant:	Description:
Math.E	Constant E, base of the natural logarithm, with an approximate value of 2.71828
Math.LN2	The natural logarithm of 2, with an approximate value of 0.69315
Math.LN10	The natural logarithm of 10, with an approximate value of 2.30259
Math.LOG2E	The base-2 logarithm of constant E, with an approximate value of 1.44269
Math.LOG10E	The base-10 logarithm of constant E, with an approximate value of 0.43429
Math.PI	The constant PI, with an approximate value of 3.14159
Math.SQRT1_2	The square root of 0.5, with an approximate value of 0.70711
Math.SQRT2	The square root of 2, with an approximate value of 1.41421

There is no need to create an instance of the Math object as it is globally available by default, so Math constants and methods are accessible from anywhere in a script via the Math object and dot syntax. Math constants are mostly used in scripts that have a particular mathematical purpose but all the Math constants are listed above for completeness.

① Create an HTML document that embeds an external script file and contains an element in which to write

```
<script type = "text/javascript" src = "constants.js" >
</script> <div id = "panel" > </div>
```

constants.html

② Create the JavaScript file with an "init" function to initialize two variables when the document has loaded

```
function init()
{
  var panel = document.getElementById( "panel" ) ;
  var rad = 4 ;
}
document.addEventListener( "DOMContentLoaded", init, false ) ;
```

constants.js

③ Next, in the function block, insert statements to declare and initialize two variables using Math object constants

```
var area = Math.PI * ( rad * rad ) ;        // ∏r²
var circ = 2  * ( Math.PI * rad ) ;         // 2∏r
```

④ Now, in the function block insert statements to write the value of each variable in the panel

```
panel.innerHTML = "Circle Radius: " + rad + " feet" ;
panel.innerHTML +=
        "<br>Area: " + area + " square feet" ;
panel.innerHTML +=
        "<br>Circumference: " + circ + " feet" ;
```

⑤ Save the script alongside the HTML document then open the page in your browser to see the variable values

Beware

All Math constant names must be stated in uppercase – for example, be sure to use **Math.PI** rather than **Math.pi**.

69

Comparing numbers

The built-in Math object provides these useful methods:

Method:	Returns:
Math.abs()	An absolute value
Math.acos()	An arc cosine value
Math.asin()	An arc sine value
Math.atan()	An arc tangent value
Math.atan2()	An angle from an X-axis point
Math.ceil()	A rounded-up value
Math.cos()	A cosine value
Math.exp()	An exponent of constant E
Math.floor()	A rounded-down value
Math.log()	A natural logarithm value
Math.max()	The larger of two numbers
Math.min()	The smaller of two numbers
Math.pow()	A power value
Math.random()	A pseudo-random number
Math.round()	The nearest integer value
Math.sin()	A sine value
Math.sqrt()	A square root value
Math.tan()	A tangent value

1 Create an HTML document that embeds an external script file and contains an element in which to write
<script type = "text/javascript" src = "math.js" >
</script> <div id = "panel" > </div>

math.html

2 Create the JavaScript file with an "init" function to initialize a variable when the document has loaded
```
function init()
{
  var panel = document.getElementById( "panel" ) ;
}
document.addEventListener( "DOMContentLoaded", init, false ) ;
```

math.js

3 Next, in the function block, insert statements to declare and initialize two more variables using Math object methods
var sq = Math.pow(5 , 2) ; // 5 to the power 2 (5 x 5).
var cb = Math.pow(4 , 3) ; // 4 to the power 3(4 x 4 x 4).

4 Now, in the function block, insert statements to write values computed by Math methods in the panel
```
panel.innerHTML =
        "Largest Positive: " + Math.max( sq , cb ) ;
panel.innerHTML +=
        "<br>Smallest Positive: " + Math.min( sq , cb ) ;
panel.innerHTML +=
     "<br>Largest Negative: " + Math.max( -5 , -4.75 ) ;
```

5 Save the script alongside the HTML document then open the page in your browser to see the computed values

Don't forget

The largest negative value is the one closest to zero.

Rounding floating-points

The built-in JavaScript Math object provides three methods for rounding floating-point numbers to integer values. Each method takes the floating-point value as its argument and returns an integer. The **Math.ceil()** method rounds up, the **Math.floor()** method rounds down, and the **Math.round()** method rounds up or down to the nearest integer.

When handling floating-point values it is important to recognize a discrepancy that exists between the prevailing computer floating-point math standard, as defined by the IEEE (Institute of Electrical and Electronics Engineers), and generally accepted mathematical accuracy. This exists because some decimal numbers cannot be exactly translated into binary form. For example, the decimal number 81.66 cannot be exactly translated to binary so the expression **15 * 81.66** returns **1224.8999999999998** rather than the mathematically accurate figure of **1224.9**.

Some programming languages provide automatic rounding to overcome floating-point discrepancies but JavaScript does not so care must be taken, especially with monetary values, to avoid mathematically erroneous results. The recommended procedure is to first multiply the floating-point value by 100, then perform the arithmetical operation, and finally divide the result by 100 to return to the same decimal level.

A similar procedure can be used to commute long floating-point values to just two decimal places. After multiplying a value by 100 the **Math.round()** method can be employed to round the value, then division by 100 returns to two decimal places.

Procedures that multiply, operate, then divide, can be written as individual steps or parentheses can be used to determine the order in a single succinct expression. For example, commuting a long floating point value in a variable named "num" can be written as:

```
var num *= 100 ;
num= Math.round( num ) ;
num /= 100 ;
```

or alternatively as:

```
var num = ( Math.round( num * 100 ) ) / 100 ;
```

① Create an HTML document that embeds an external script file and contains an element in which to write
<script type = "text/javascript" src = "float.js" > </script> <div id = "panel" > </div>

float.html

float.js

② Create the JavaScript file with an "init" function to initialize a variable and write various rounded values in the panel
function init()
{
  var panel = document.getElementById("panel") ;
  panel.innerHTML = "Ceiling: " + Math.ceil(7.5) +
  **"
Floor: " + Math.floor(7.5) + "
Round+: " +**
  **Math.round(7.5) + "
Round-: " + Math.round(-7.5) ;**
}
document.addEventListener("DOMContentLoaded", init, false) ;

③ Next, in the function block, insert statements to write values showing and correcting a floating-point discrepancy
panel.innerHTML += "<hr>Inprecision: " + (81.66 * 15)
**+ "
Corrected: " + ((81.66 * 100) * 15) / 100 ;**

④ Now, in the function block, insert statements to write values showing and commuting a long floating-point value
panel.innerHTML +=
**"<hr>Float: " + Math.PI + "
Commuted: "**
+ (Math.round(Math.PI * 100)) / 100 ;

⑤ Save the script alongside the HTML document then open the page in your browser to see the computed values

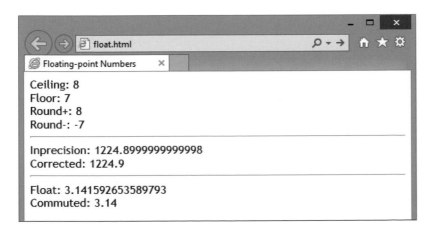

Floating-point Numbers

Ceiling: 8
Floor: 7
Round+: 8
Round-: -7

Inprecision: 1224.8999999999998
Corrected: 1224.9

Float: 3.141592653589793
Commuted: 3.14

Don't forget

Expressions in innermost parentheses are evaluated first.

93

Generating random numbers

The JavaScript **Math.random()** method returns a random floating-point number between 0.0 and 1.0. This can be used for a variety of web page effects such as random banner rotation or random lottery number selection.

Multiplying the random floating-point value will increase its range. For example, multiplying it by 10 increases the range to become 0.0–10.0.

Generally, it is useful to round the random value up with the **Math.ceil()** method so that the range becomes 1–10.

The process of specifying the range for a random number value can be written as individual steps or parentheses can be used to determine the order in a single succinct expression. For example, specifying a range of 1–10 for a variable named "rand" can be written as:

```
var rand = Math.random() ;
rand *= 10 ;
rand = Math.ceil( rand ) ;
```

or alternatively as:

```
var rand = Math.ceil( Math.random() * 10 ) ;
```

random.html

random.js

① Create an HTML document that embeds an external script file and contains an element in which to write
```
<script type="text/javascript" src="random.js"></script>
<div id="panel"> </div>
```

② Create the JavaScript file with an "init" function to initialize a variable and declare other variables – including one array variable
```
function init()
{
  var panel = document.getElementById( "panel" ) ;
  var i , rand , temp , str , nums = [] ;
}
document.addEventListener("DOMContentLoaded", init, false );
```

③ Next, in the function block, fill array elements 1–49 with their respective index number

```
for ( i = 1 ; i < 50 ; i++ )
{
  nums[ i ] = i ;
}
```

④ Now, in the function block, randomize the numbers in the elements

```
for ( i = 1 ; i < 50 ; i++ )
{
  rand = Math.ceil( Math.random() * 49 ) ;
  temp = nums[ i ] ;
  nums[ i ] = nums[ rand ] ;
  nums[ rand ] = temp ;
}
```

Hot tip

Step 4 contains a sort algorithm that ensures no two elements contain the same number.

⑤ Finally, in the function block, write a string in the panel including the numbers from array elements 1–6

```
str = "Your Six Lucky Numbers:<br>" ;
for ( i = 1 ; i < 7 ; i++ )
{
  str += nums[ i ] ;
  if( i !== 6 ) { str += " - " ; }
}
panel.innerHTML = str ;
```

⑥ Save the script alongside the HTML document then open the page in your browser to see six random numbers in the range 1–49

Your Six Lucky Numbers:
37 - 24 - 45 - 16 - 38 - 7

Uniting strings

JavaScript has a String object that provides useful methods to manipulate string values. There is, however, no need to create instances of the String object, with the **new** keyword and **String()** constructor, as its methods can simply be applied to string variables using dot syntax. For example, **str.toUpperCase()** returns all characters of a string variable named "str" in uppercase, whereas **str.toLowerCase()** returns all its characters in lowercase.

There is also a string **length** property that stores the total number of characters in a string.

Many of the examples listed earlier use the **+** concatenation operator to unite multiple strings but, alternatively, the string **concat()** method can be used to append one or more strings supplied as a comma-separated list of arguments.

The internal **eval()** method is also used to unite strings and variables by some script authors – but this should be avoided. Typically, it is found to be referencing some part of a document by combining a property, ID, and value using dot syntax like this:

eval("document.images." + picID + ".src = ' " + picFile + " ' ") ;

A much better solution is to reference the item using subscript notation, rather than dot syntax, where each property name is a string between square brackets – so the example above becomes:

document.images[picID].src = picFile ;

This automatically substitutes the string values so might equate to:

document.images["myPicID"] .src = "myPicFile.png" ;

The **eval()** method directly calls the JavaScript compiler to compile its argument into a JavaScript statement which it then executes. This incurs a large cost in script performance and is unnecessary in almost every case as there is usually a more efficient and elegant solution. Furthermore, the **eval()** method can have security implications if it allows user input to be evaluated as a JavaScript instruction.

1 Create an HTML document that embeds an external script file and contains an element in which to write

```
<script type = "text/javascript" src = "string.js" >
</script> <div id = "panel" > </div>
```

string.html

2 Create the JavaScript file with an "init" function to initialize some variables

```
function init()
{
  var panel = document.getElementById( "panel" ) ;
  var s1 = "JavaScript" , s2 = " in Easy " , s3 = "Steps" ;
  var picName = "myPic" , picFile = "poolballs.png" ;
}
document.addEventListener( "DOMContentLoaded", init, false ) ;
```

string.js

3 Next, in the function block, insert statements to write manipulated string values in the panel

```
panel.innerHTML = s1.toUpperCase() ;
panel.innerHTML += "<br>" + s1.toLowerCase() ;
panel.innerHTML += "<br>" + s1.concat( s2 , s3 ) ;
panel.innerHTML +=
    "<br>" + s1 + " has " + s1.length + " characters" ;
```

4 Now, in the function block, insert statements to write an image into the panel using subscript notation

```
panel.innerHTML += "<br><img id = 'myPic' >" ;
document.images[ picName ].src = picFile ;
```

5 Save the script alongside the HTML document then open the page in your browser to see the strings and the image

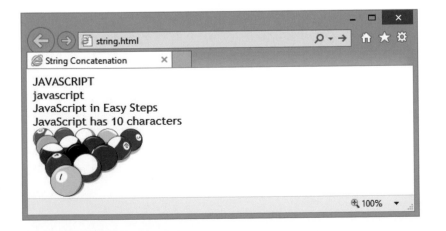

Don't forget

Use single quotes for strings nested within outer strings that are contained within double quotes.

Splitting strings

There are several string methods that allow a specified part of a string to be copied from the full string. These treat each string like an array, in which each element contains a character or a space, and can be referenced by their index position. As with arrays the string index is zero-based, so the first character is at position zero.

The start at which to begin copying a "substring" can be specified by stating its index position as an argument to the string's **substring()** method. This will copy all characters after that position right up to the end of the string. Optionally, a second argument may be supplied to the string's **substring()** method to specify a subsequent index position as the end of the substring. This will then copy all characters between the start and end positions.

An alternative way to copy substrings is provided by the string **substr()** method. Like the **substring()** method this can take a single argument to specify the index position at which to begin copying and will copy all characters after that position right up to the end of the string. Unlike the **substring()** method, the **substr()** method may optionally be supplied with a second argument to specify the number of characters to copy after the start position.

Similarly, the string **slice()** method can be used to return all characters after a start position, specified by a single argument, or all characters between two positions, specified as two arguments.

It is sometimes useful to copy parts of a string that are separated by a particular character. The separator character can be specified as an argument to the string **split()** method, which will return an array of all substrings that exist between occurrences of that character. Optionally the **split()** method may be supplied with a second argument specifying the size of the array it should return. In this case each substring that exists between the specified separator character is returned until the limit is reached, and the rest of the string is ignored.

None of these string methods modify the original string but merely make a copy of a particular part of the original string.

① Create an HTML document that embeds an external script file and contains an element in which to write
`<script type = "text/javascript" src = "substring.js" > </script> <div id = "panel" > </div>`

substring.html

② Create the JavaScript file with an "init" function to initialize two variables
```
function init()
{
  var panel = document.getElementById( "panel" ) ;
  var dfn = "JavaScript is the original dialect of the
  ECMAScript standard language whereas JScript is the
  dialect developed later by Microsoft." ;
}
document.addEventListener( "DOMContentLoaded", init, false ) ;
```

substring.js

③ Next, in the function block, insert statements to write various copied substrings in the panel
```
panel.innerHTML = dfn.slice( 0 , 26 ) ;
panel.innerHTML += dfn.slice( 61 , 70 ) + "<br>" ;

panel.innerHTML += dfn.split( " " , 4 ) + "<br>" ;

panel.innerHTML += dfn.substring( 79 , 94 ) ;
panel.innerHTML += dfn.substring( 121 , 130 ) ;

panel.innerHTML += dfn.substr( 61 , 10 ) ;
```

⑤ Save the script alongside the HTML document then open the page in your browser to see the substrings

```
┌─────────────────────────────────────────────┐
│ ⬅ ➡  📄 substring.html        🔎 ▾ → 🏠 ★ ☼ │
│ 🌐 Extracting Substrings    ✕               │
│ JavaScript is the original language          │
│ JavaScript,is,the,original                   │
│ JScript is the Microsoft language            │
│                                              │
│                                              │
│                                 🔍 100% ▾    │
└─────────────────────────────────────────────┘
```

Don't forget

Specify "" (an empty string without any space) as the separator to the split function to return an array of individual characters.

Finding characters

The JavaScript String object provides a number of methods that allow a string to be searched for a particular character or substring. The string **search()** method takes a substring as its argument and returns the position at which that occurs in the searched string, or a -1 if it is not found. Alternatively, the substring can be specified as the argument to the string **match()** method that will return the substring if it is present, or the JavaScript **null** value if it is absent.

The string **indexOf()** method takes a substring as its argument and returns the index position of the first occurrence of the substring when it's present, or -1 when it's absent. The **lastIndexOf()** method works in the same way but searches backwards, from the end of the string, reporting the last occurrence of the substring.

To discover the character at a particular index position in a string, its index value can be specified as an argument to the **charAt()** method, or its numerical Unicode value can be revealed by specifying its index value to the **charCodeAt()** method. Conversely one or more Unicode values can be specified as arguments to the **String.fromCharCode()** method to return their character values.

Additionally, all occurrences of a character or substring can be replaced by specifying their value as the first argument to the string **replace()** method, and a replacement value as its second argument.

Beware

The **null** keyword is not equivalent to a zero value, as **null** has no value whatsoever.

search.html

search.js

1 Create an HTML document that embeds an external script file and contains an element in which to write
<script type = "text/javascript" src = "search.js" > </script> <div id = "panel" > </div>

2 Create the JavaScript file with an "init" function to declare and initialize two variables
function init()
{
  var panel = document.getElementById("panel") ;
  var str = "JavaScript in easy steps" ;
}
document.addEventListener("DOMContentLoaded", init, false) ;

3 Next, in the function block, insert statements to search for a substring
```
panel.innerHTML = "'Script' search: " + str.search( "Script" ) ;
panel.innerHTML +=
        "<br>'Script' match: " + str.match( "Script" ) ;
```

4 Now, in the function block, insert statements to search for a character
```
panel.innerHTML += "<br>indexOf 's': " + str.indexOf( "s" ) ;
panel.innerHTML +=
        "<br>lastIndexOf 's': " + str.lastIndexOf( "s" ) ;
```

Hot tip

Unicode uppercase A–Z values are 65-90 and lowercase a–z values are 97–122.

5 Insert statements to search by index position and write character equivalents of Unicode values
```
panel.innerHTML += "<br>charAt 0: " + str.charAt( 0 ) ;
panel.innerHTML +=
        "<br>charCodeAt 0: " + str.charCodeAt( 0 ) ;
panel.innerHTML += "<br>fromCharCode: " +
        String.fromCharCode( 74 , 97 , 118 , 97 ) ;
```

6 Finally, insert a statement to replace a substring with an alternative substring
```
panel.innerHTML+=
        "<br>replace: " + str.replace( "easy" , "simple" ) ;
```

7 Save the script alongside the HTML document then open the page in your browser to see the result of each search

Don't forget

The **replace()** method returns a modified version of the original string but does not actually change the original string.

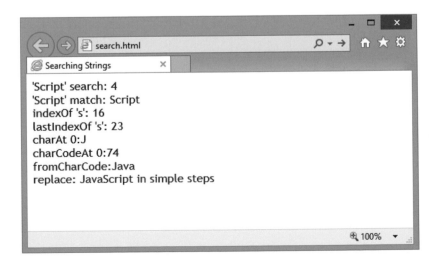

Getting numbers from strings

JavaScript has three top-level internal functions that are useful to determine if a value is not a number (**NaN**) and to extract numerical values from the beginning of string values.

The internal **isNaN()** function takes a value as its argument and returns **true** if that argument is not a numerical value, otherwise it returns **false**. This test may seem somewhat paradoxical but it is simpler, and therefore more efficient, to examine what something is not – rather than what something is. For example, the color maroon is plainly not green – but is it a kind of red? Of course the function can be prefixed by the unary **!** NOT operator to reverse the intent, so that **!isNaN()** returns **true** when the argument is indeed a numerical value.

The internal **parseInt()** function is very useful as it examines a string supplied as its first argument and returns an integer copied from the start of the string if possible. Where the string begins with a non-numerical value **parseInt()** returns the **NaN** value. By default, the number in the string is assumed to be decimal unless it begins with a 0 (zero), indicating an octal number, or begins with 0X indicating a hexadecimal number.

To avoid confusion **parseInt()** can, optionally, take a second argument that is a "radix" value specifying the base of the numbering system to be used. It is recommended that a radix is always explicitly supplied to the **parseInt()** function to prevent unintentional errors. For example, if **parseInt()** was examining a user input value without a radix the function would automatically regard any input numerical value beginning with 0 as octal – even when the script requests a decimal value from the user.

There is also an internal **parseFloat()** function that examines a string argument and returns a floating-point number copied from the start of the string if possible. Where the string begins with a non-numerical value **parseFloat()** returns the **NaN** value. Unlike **parseInt()** the floating-point number returned by **parseFloat()** will always be decimal so there is no question of the numbering system.

① Create an HTML document that embeds an external script file and contains an element in which to write
```
<script type = "text/javascript" src = "parse.js" >
</script> <div id = "panel" > </div>
```

parse.html

② Create the JavaScript file with an "init" function to initialize two variables
```
function init()
{
  var panel = document.getElementById( "panel" ) ;
  var num = "074.5 Input" ;
}
document.addEventListener( "DOMContentLoaded", init, false ) ;
```

parse.js

③ Next, in the function block, insert statements to examine the data type of a variable and write the results in the panel
```
panel.innerHTML += "Not a number?: " + isNaN( num ) ;
panel.innerHTML += "<br>This value is a " + typeof num ;
```

④ Now, in the function block, insert statements to copy integers from the start of a string using different numbering systems
```
panel.innerHTML += "<hr>Octal: " + parseInt( num , 8 )
+ "<br>Decimal: " + parseInt( num , 10 )
+ "<br>Hexadecimal: " + parseInt( num , 16 ) ;
```

⑤ Finally, in the function block, insert a statement to copy a floating-point value from the start of the string
```
panel.innerHTML += "<br>Float: " + parseFloat( num ) ;
```

⑥ Save the script alongside the HTML document then open the page in your browser to see the extracted numbers

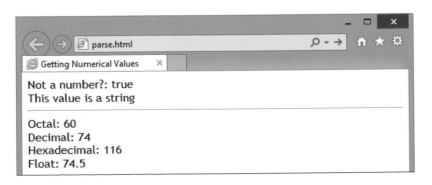

Summary

- The largest and smallest of two numbers can be discovered by the **Math.max()** and **Math.min()** methods

- Floating-point numbers can be rounded to a near integer with the **Math.ceil()**, **Math.floor()**, and **Math.round()** methods

- The **Math.random()** method returns a floating-point number between 0.0 and 1.0, which can be multiplied and rounded to specify a range of random integer numbers

- The built-in String object has a **length** property that stores the number of characters in a string

- Character case can be modified with the string **toUpperCase()** and **toLowerCase()** methods

- The internal **eval()** method should be avoided as it is usually inefficient and can have security implications

- String methods treat each string as an array of characters that can be referenced by their index position

- The **substring()** and **substr()** methods can be used to copy sections of a string

- A string can be separated into an array of substrings by specifying a separator character to the **split()** method

- The **search()**, **match()**, and **indexOf()** methods can be used to search a string for the presence of a specified substring

- A substring can be replaced using the **replace()** method

- The internal **isNaN()** function evaluates its argument to determine whether it has a numerical value

- The internal **parseInt()** and **parseFloat()** methods return a numerical value from the start of a specified string argument

- A radix argument should always be supplied to the internal **parseInt()** function to specify which numbering system to use

7

Referencing the window object

This chapter demonstrates how to use properties and methods of the window object from the Document Object Model (DOM).

Introducing the DOM

The browser represents all components of a web page within a hierarchical tree called the Document Object Model (DOM). Each component appears below the top-level **window** object, and the tree typically contains the branches illustrated below:

Hot tip

Items followed by square brackets are array objects, and those within regular parentheses are all the different possible types of form elements.

Beware

The **window.event** object is present in the Internet Explorer DOM but absent in Mozilla-based browsers such as Firefox.

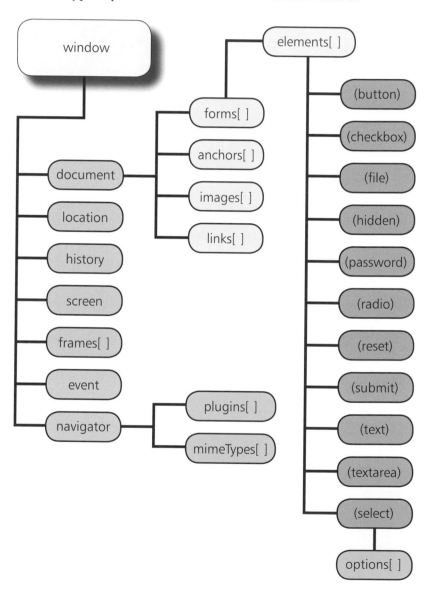

A **for in** loop can be used to list all properties of the window object provided by the browser. The list will contain fundamental properties that are common to all modern browsers plus minor properties that are browser-specific.

① Create an HTML document that embeds an external script file and contains an element in which to write
```
<script type = "text/javascript" src = "dom.js" > </script>
<div id = "panel" > </div>
```

dom.html

② Create the JavaScript file with an "init" function to initialize a variable and declare a second variable
```
function init()
{
  var panel = document.getElementById( "panel" ) ;
  var property ;
}
document.addEventListener( "DOMContentLoaded", init, false ) ;
```

dom.js

③ Next, in the function block, insert a loop to list each property within the DOM window object
```
for ( property in window )
{
  if ( property ) { panel.innerHTML += property + " , " ; }
}
```

④ Save the script alongside the HTML document then open the page in a browser to see the window object properties

107

Don't forget

The **window** properties are provided by the browser so will vary by browser and version.

Inspecting window properties

The top-level DOM **window** object has a **screen** child object that provides properties describing the user's monitor resolution in pixel measurement. Overall screen dimensions can be found in the **screen.width** and **screen.height** properties whereas the usable dimensions, excluding the space occupied by the task bar, can be found in the **screen.availWidth** and **screen.availHeight** properties.

The screen's color capability can be discovered from the **screen.colorDepth** property that contains the bit value describing the range of possible colors that screen can display. A Low Color 8-bit value can display just 256 colors, a High Color 16-bit value can display 65,536 colors, a 24-bit True Color value can display millions of colors, and a 32-bit Deep Color value can display a gamut comprising a billion or more colors.

A default message to be displayed on the window's status bar can be specified by assigning a string to the **window.defaultStatus** property. At other times the default message can be replaced by a different string assigned to the **window.status** property. These can be used to advise the user on the progress of a script application but should not be relied upon, as the user may have disabled status bar messages or removed the status bar from the browser window.

Beware

Notice the "camel case" capitalization of these property names.

window.html

window.js

1. Create an HTML document that embeds an external script file and contains an element in which to write
   <script type = "text/javascript" src = "window.js" > </script><div id = "panel" > </div>

2. Create the JavaScript file with an "init" function to initialize a variable and declare other variables to store screen properties
   function init()
   {
     var panel = document.getElementById("panel") ;
     var width , height , avWidth , avHeight , colors ;
   }
   document.addEventListener("DOMContentLoaded", init, false) ;

3   Next, in the function block, assign screen properties to variables

```
width = window.screen.width ;
height = window.screen.height ;
avWidth = window.screen.availWidth ;
avHeight = window.screen.availHeight ;
```

4   Now, examine the color bit value and assign an appropriate string value to a variable

```
switch( window.screen.colorDepth )
{
  case 8 : colors = "Low Color" ; break ;
  case 16 : colors = "High Color" ; break ;
  case 24 : colors = "True Color" ; break ;
  case 32 : colors = "Deep Color" ; break ;
  default : colors = "Unknown" ;
}
```

> **Hot tip**
>
> The **colorDepth** property can be used to deliver low resolution images within a document for browsers with limited color capabilities.

5   Insert statements to write each variable describing screen properties in the panel

```
panel.innerHTML = "Screen Resolution: " + width +
                    " x " + height + "<br>" ;
panel.innerHTML += "Available Screen Size: " + avWidth +
                    " x " + avHeight + "<br>" ;
panel.innerHTML += "Color Capability: " + colors ;
```

6   Finally, in the function block, assign a default status bar message

```
window.defaultStatus = "Screen Data by JavaScript" ;
```

7   Save the script alongside the HTML document then open the page in a browser to see the window screen properties and default status bar message

109

Displaying dialog messages

The top-level DOM **window** object provides three methods with which JavaScript can display dialog messages to the user. A simple warning message string can be specified as the argument to the **window.alert()** method. This gets displayed in a dialog box with just an "OK" button, which merely closes the dialog box.

More usefully, a message can be specified as the argument to the **window.confirm()** method to request a decision from the user. This gets displayed in a dialog box with an "OK" button and a "Cancel" button. Either button will close the dialog box when pushed but the "OK" button returns a **true** value, whereas the "Cancel" button returns a **false** value.

A message can also be specified as the argument to the **window.prompt()** method to request input from the user. This gets displayed in a dialog box with an "OK" button, a "Cancel" button, and a text input field. Either button will close the dialog box when pushed but the "OK" button returns the value in the text field, whereas the "Cancel" button returns a **null** value. Optionally, a second argument can be supplied to the **window.prompt()** method to specify default content for the text field.

dialog.html

dialog.js

Create an HTML document that embeds an external script file and contains an element in which to write
<script type = "text/javascript" src = "dialog.js" > </script> <div id = "panel" > </div>

Create the JavaScript file with an "init" function to initialize a variable when the document has loaded
function init()
{
 var panel = document.getElementById("panel") ;
}
document.addEventListener("DOMContentLoaded", init, false) ;

Next, in the function block, insert a statement to display a message in a simple dialog box
window.alert("Here's a simple message.") ;

Now, in the function block, insert a statement to request a decision from the user and write the result in the panel
panel.innerHTML =
  "Confirm: " + window.confirm("Go or Stop?") ;

5 Finally, in the function block, insert a statement to request text input from the user and write the returned text into the panel
**panel.innerHTML += "
Prompt: " +**
window.prompt("Yes or No?" , "Yes") ;

6 Save the script alongside the HTML document then open the page in your browser and push the "OK" button on each dialog as they appear

Hot tip

The **confirm** dialog can be used with an **if** statement to branch a script. For example, **if(confirm("OK?")) {...} else {...};**

Scrolling and moving position

The DOM **window** object has a **scrollBy()** method that allows the window to be scrolled horizontally and vertically when content overflows the window in either orientation. This method requires two arguments to specify the number of pixels to shift along the X and Y axes.

When content overflows the window vertically, so a scroll bar appears along the right edge of the browser window, the **scrollBy()** method will scroll by the number of pixels specified as its first argument – or until it reaches the extreme of the content.

Similarly, when content overflows the window horizontally, so a scroll bar appears along the bottom of the browser window, the **scrollBy()** method will scroll by the number of pixels specified as its second argument – or until it reaches the extreme of the content.

There is also a **scrollTo()** method that accepts two arguments specifying X and Y coordinates that the top left corner of the window should scroll to when content overflows the window horizontally and vertically. This can be used to shift away from the default X=0, Y=0 coordinates to a specified alternative position. For example, where the browser is displaying data in a tabular spreadsheet format, with the first cell of the first row in the top left corner of the browser window, the **scrollTo()** method can place a particular cell at the top left corner of the browser window instead.

A browser window that occupies the entire desktop space typically has its top left corner at X=0, Y=0 coordinates of the screen, but smaller browser windows can, of course, be dragged to any screen coordinates. The position on the screen of smaller browser windows can also be determined in script by specifying X and Y screen axes coordinates to the **moveTo()** method. For example, this method can be used to move the window to the top left corner of the screen by specifying zero coordinates for each axis.

There is also a **moveBy()** method that accepts two arguments to specify how many pixels along the X and Y axes the window position should be shifted from its current screen position.

Hot tip

Supply negative values to the **scrollBy()** and **moveBy()** methods to move up and left.

Beware

The effect of the **scrollBy()** method is only apparent when the content overflows the window – causing scroll bars to appear.

1. Create an HTML document that embeds an external script file and contains an element in which to write
```
<script type = "text/javascript" src = "scroll.js" >
</script> <div id = "panel" > </div>
```

scroll.html

2. Create the JavaScript file with an "init" function to declare a counter variable and to initialize a second variable
```
function init()
{
  var i , panel = document.getElementById( "panel" ) ;
}
document.addEventListener( "DOMContentLoaded", init, false ) ;
```

scroll.js

3. Next, in the function block, insert a loop to write five hundred numbers in the panel, to make the window content overflow
```
for ( i = 1 ; i < 501 ; i++ ) { panel.innerHTML +=  i + " " ; }
```

4. Now, in the function block, add statements to scroll down by 500 pixels and position the window at the top left of the screen
```
window.scrollBy( 0 , 500 ) ;
window.moveTo( 0 , 0 ) ;
```

5. Save the script alongside the HTML document then open the page in a browser window that is not full-screen size to see the window scroll and move

113

Opening new windows

A new browser window can be opened using the **window** object's **open()** method that requires three string arguments. The first argument is the URL address of the HTML document to be loaded in the new window, the second argument is simply a name for the new window, and the third argument is a comma-separated list of features that the window should include – from the possible features described in the table below:

Feature:	Description:
directories	Adds the links bar
height	Sets height in pixels of the document area
left	The screen X coordinate of the window
location	Adds the address bar
menubar	Adds the standard menu bar
resizable	Permits the window to be resized
scrollbars	Enables scrollbars when needed
status	Adds the status bar
toolbar	Adds the Forward and Back buttons bar
top	The screen Y coordinate of the window
width	Sets width in pixels of the document area

Don't forget

Browser makers have added Popup Blockers due to the annoying proliferation of popup windows – so the use of popups is no longer recommended, but they are demonstrated here for completeness.

When successful the **window.open()** method returns a new **window** object and opens the new "popup" window in front of the old window. If it fails the method simply returns **null**. In either event the returned result should be assigned to a variable which may be subsequently tested – if the variable is not **null** it must then represent the popup window object. That window may then be closed by calling its **close()** method, or its contents printed by calling its **print()** method, using the variable name and dot syntax. For example, where the result of the **window.open()** method is assigned to a variable named "win" that window can be closed by calling **win.close()**.

1 Create an HTML document that embeds an external script file and contains an element in which to write
<script type = "text/javascript" src = "popup.js" > </script> <div id = "panel" > </div>

popup.html

2 Also create a second HTML document named "pop.html" to be displayed in a popup window
<p>Extra Information in this Popup Window</p>

pop.html

3 Create the JavaScript file with an "init" function to declare a variable and write a simple message in the panel
function init()
{
  var panel = document.getElementById("panel") ;
  panel.innerHTML =
      "Regular information in the main window" ;
}
document.addEventListener("DOMContentLoaded", init, false) ;

popup.js

4 Next, in the function block, declare a second variable and assign it the result of attempting to open a popup window
var winObject = window.open("pop.html" , "windowName" , "top=200,left=100,width=450,height=100,status=yes") ;

5 Save the script alongside the HTML documents then open a web browser and turn off Popup Blocker features

6 Now, open the web page in your browser to see the popup window appear in front of the main window

Beware

Do not put any spaces in the features list string as it may cause the **window.open()** method to fail.

Making a window timer

The JavaScript **window** object has an interesting **setTimeout()** method that can repeatedly evaluate a specified expression after a specified period of time. Where the specified expression calls the function in which the **window.setTimout()** statement appears a recursive loop is created – in which the function is repeatedly executed after the specified period of time.

The expression to be evaluated by the **setTimeout()** method must be specified as its first argument and the period of time must be a number specified as its second argument. The time is expressed in milliseconds, where 1000 represents one second.

The **setTimeout()** method returns a numeric value that can be assigned to a variable to uniquely identify the waiting process. This value can be specified as the argument to the window object's **clearTimeout()** method to terminate the timer loop at some point.

The **window** object also has **setInterval()** and **clearInterval()** methods that take the same arguments and work in a similar way. The difference is that the time specified to the **setInterval()** method specifies the interval at which point the expression is to be evaluated irrespective of how long it takes to execute. Conversely, the time specified to the **setTimeout()** method specifies the period of time between the end of one execution until the start of the next execution. This means that it is possible for the **setInterval()** method to attempt overlapping executions where the interval is short and the time taken to execute the expression is lengthy. For this reason it is generally preferable to use the **setTimeout()** method.

timer.html

timer.js

1. Create an HTML document that embeds an external script file and contains an element in which to write
```
<script type = "text/javascript" src = "timer.js" >
</script>
<div id = "panel" > </div>
```

2. Create the JavaScript file and initialize a global counter variable at zero
```
var counter = 0 ;
```

3 Next, add an "init" function to declare two variables
```
function init()
{
  var timerId , panel = document.getElementById( "panel" ) ;
}
document.addEventListener( "DOMContentLoaded", init, false ) ;
```

4 Now, in the function block, increment the counter variable
```
counter++ ;
```

5 Next, in the function block, write a span element in the panel to display the current value of the counter variable
```
panel.innerHTML += "<span style='background:black;
    color;white;margin:2px;'>" + counter + "</span>" ;
```

6 Insert a statement to terminate the loop when the counter value reaches 20 or repeat if it's less than 20
```
if ( counter > 19 )
{ window.clearTimeout( timerId ) ; }
else
{ timerId = window.setTimeout( init , 1000 ) ; }
```

7 Save the script alongside the HTML document then open the page in your browser to see the spans get added each second until the counter reaches 20

Beware

Notice that the style rules are enclosed within single quotes to avoid conflict with the outer double quotes.

Querying the browser

In the DOM hierarchy the top-level **window** object has a number of child objects, which each have their own properties and methods. One of these is the **window.navigator** object that contains information about the web browser. As the top-level **window** object exists in the "global namespace" all its child objects can omit that part of the address so the **window.alert()** method can be simply called using **alert()**, the **window.onload** property can be referenced using **onload**, and so the **window.navigator** object can be referenced using **navigator**.

The **navigator** object has an **appName** property that contains the browser name, an **appCodeName** property that contains its code name, and an **appVersion** property that contains its version number. But you may be surprised with the values as Internet Explorer, Firefox, Safari, and Opera all give their code name as "Mozilla".

Each browser sends the browser code name and version in an HTTP header named "User-Agent" when making a request to a web server, and this string can also be retrieved from the **navigator.userAgent** property. There is also a **navigator.platform** property that describes the browser's host operating system.

In previous years much was made of browser detection scripts that attempted to identify the browser using its **navigator** properties so that appropriate code could be supplied to suit that browser's supported features. This is now considered bad practice and it is now recommended that feature detection be used instead.

For example, querying if the browser supports the useful **document.addEventListener()** method determines whether that browser supports the modern Document Object Model.

browser.html

browser.js

1 Create an HTML document that embeds an external script file and contains an element in which to write
```
<script type = "text/javascript" src = "browser.js" >
</script> <div id = "panel" > </div>
```

2 Create the JavaScript file with an "init" function to initialize a variable when the document has loaded
```
function init()
{
  var panel = document.getElementById( "panel" ) ;
}
document.addEventListener( "DOMContentLoaded", init, false ) ;
```

3 In the function block, insert statements to write the browser properties and host system type in the panel
panel.innerHTML += "Browser: " + navigator.appName ;
panel.innerHTML +=
       "\<br\>Code Name: " + navigator.appCodeName ;
panel.innerHTML +=
       "\<br\>Version: " + navigator.appVersion ;
panel.innerHTML +=
       "\<br\>Platform: " + navigator.platform ;

4 Next, in the function block, insert a statement to write a message in the panel if support of a modern DOM method is detected
if (document.addEventListener)
{ panel.innerHTML += "This is a Modern DOM Browser" ; }

5 Save the script alongside the HTML document then open the page in different browsers to compare their properties

119

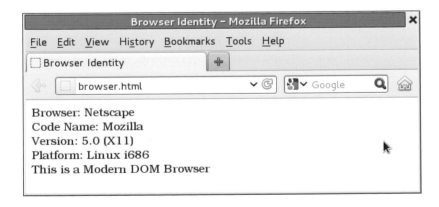

Discovering what is enabled

The DOM **window** object's **navigator** child object has a **javaEnabled()** method that will return **true** only if Java support is enabled in the web browser. Additionally, **navigator** has a **plugins** child object and a **mimeTypes** child object. Neither of these two objects is implemented in Internet Explorer but in Mozilla browsers, such as Firefox, each is an array in which every element contains details of a supported feature.

As with other arrays, the **plugins** and **mimeTypes** arrays both have a **length** property containing the numeric total of their elements.

Each **plugin** array element has a **name** and **description** property containing details of one installed plugin feature. These can be referenced using the element index number as usual. For example, **navigator.plugins[0].name** references the **name** property of the first element in the **plugins** array.

Similarly, each **mimeTypes** array element has a **type** and **description** property containing details of one supported MIME feature. These can be referenced using the element index number as usual. For example, **navigator.mimeTypes[0].type** references the **type** property of the first element in the **mimeTypes** array.

Don't forget

The contents of these array elements vary according to which features are supported by each browser.

120

enabled.html

enabled.js

1 Create an HTML document that embeds an external script file and contains an element in which to write
```
<script type = "text/javascript" src = "enabled.js">
</script>
<div id = "panel" > </div>
```

2 Create the JavaScript file with an "init" function to initialize a variable when the document has loaded
```
function init()
{
  var panel = document.getElementById( "panel" ) ;
}
document.addEventListener( "DOMContentLoaded", init, false ) ;
```

3 Next, in the function block, insert a statement to write a message in the panel only if Java support is enabled
```
if ( navigator.javaEnabled() )
{
  panel.innerHTML = "Java Support is Enabled" ;
}
```

4 Now, in the function block, insert statements to write the length of the plugins array and an example element

```
if ( navigator.plugins.length !== 0 )
{
  panel.innerHTML +=
        "<hr>Total Plugins: " + navigator.plugins.length ;
  panel.innerHTML +=
        "<br>Example: " + navigator.plugins[ 1 ].name ;
  panel.innerHTML +=
        " - " + navigator.plugins[ 1 ].description ;
}
```

Hot tip

Use loops to write all plugins and mimeTypes element contents.

5 Finally, in the function block, insert statements to write the length of the MIME types array and an example element

```
if ( navigator.mimeTypes.length !== 0 )
{
  panel.innerHTML +=
  "<hr>Total MIME Types: " + navigator.mimeTypes.length ;
  panel.innerHTML +=
  "<br>Example: " + navigator.mimeTypes[ 3 ].type ;
  panel.innerHTML +=
  " - " + navigator.mimeTypes[ 3 ].description ;
}
```

6 Save the script alongside the HTML document then open the page in the Firefox browser to see what features are enabled

Controlling location

The window's **location** object has five properties containing the components of the full URL address of the document currently loaded in the browser window. The complete address, describing the protocol, domain name, file name, and fragment anchor if applicable, is contained in the **location.href** property. Separate components of the complete address are contained in the **location.protocol** (http:), **location.host** (domain name), **location.pathname** (file name), and **location.hash** (fragment anchor). Assigning a new URL to the **location** property will cause the browser to load that page or other resource at that address.

location.html

location.js

1 Create an HTML document that embeds an external script file and contains an element in which to write
<script type = "text/javascript" src = "location.js" > </script> <div id ="panel" > </div>

2 Create the JavaScript file with an "init" function to initialize a variable when the document has loaded
function init()
{
  var panel = document.getElementById("panel") ;
}
document.addEventListener("DOMContentLoaded", init, false) ;

3 Next, in the function block, insert a statement to write a fragment anchor in the panel
panel.innerHTML =
        "<a name='frag'>Fragment Anchor</a>" ;

4 Now, in the function block, insert a statement requesting the user to confirm they wish to jump to the fragment anchor location, by concatenating the anchor name onto the current address
var jump = confirm("Jump to fragment?") ;
if (jump) { location = location.href + "#frag" ; }

5 Finally, in the function block, insert statements to write each component of the current location address in the panel
panel.innerHTML += "<hr>Href: " + location.href ;
**panel.innerHTML += "
Protocol: " + location.protocol ;**
**panel.innerHTML += "
Host: " + location.host ;**
**panel.innerHTML += "
Path: " + location.pathname ;**
**panel.innerHTML += "
Hash: " + location.hash ;**

Don't forget

A web browser can load a file of any supported MIME type. For example, all PNG image files of the MIME type image/png.

6 Save the script alongside the HTML document then open the page in your browser and push Cancel on the confirm dialog to see the location components of the page address

7 Reload the page in your browser but now push OK on the confirm dialog to see the location components of the fragment anchor address

Traveling through history

The web browser stores a history of the URLs visited in the current session as an array within the **window** object's **history** child object. Like other arrays, this has a **length** property and also **back()** and **forward()** methods to move between elements. Alternatively, the history object's **go()** method accepts a positive or negative integer argument specifying how many elements to move along the array. For example, **history.go(1)** moves forward one element, and **history.go(-2)** moves back two elements.

history-1.html
history-2.html
history-3.html

history.js

Don't forget

Button event-handlers, such as onclick, are described in much more detail on page 142.

1 Create three identical HTML documents that embed the same external script file and contain an element in which to write from JavaScript
```
<script type = "text/javascript" src = "history.js" >
</script>
<div id = "panel" >  </div>
```

2 Create the JavaScript file with an "init" function to initialize a variable when the document has loaded
```
function init()
{
    var panel = document.getElementById( "panel" ) ;
}
document.addEventListener( "DOMContentLoaded", init, false ) ;
```

3 Next, in the function block, insert statements to write hyperlinks targeting each HTML document in the panel
```
panel.innerHTML +=
        "<a href='history-1.html'>Page 1</a> | " ;
panel.innerHTML +=
        "<a href='history-2.html'>Page 2</a> | " ;
panel.innerHTML +=
        "<a href='history-3.html'>Page 3</a>" ;
```

4 Now, in the function block, insert statements to write the browser's history length and current document in the panel
```
panel.innerHTML +=
        "<br>History Length: " + history.length + "<br>" ;
panel.innerHTML +=
        "Current Location: " + location.pathname + "<br>" ;
```

5 Finally, in the function block, insert statements to create buttons that call history methods when pushed
panel.innerHTML +=
"<button onclick='history.back()'>Back</button> " ;
panel.innerHTML +=
"<button onclick='history.forward()'>Forward</button>" ;

Hot tip

The URLs are stored in the history object array elements in a protected manner so they cannot be retrieved as strings.

6 Save the script alongside the HTML document then open a page to see the initial history length is 1

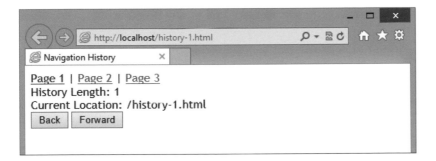

7 Click a link to load another page and see the history length increment, then click the Back button to return to the first page but see the history length remain the same

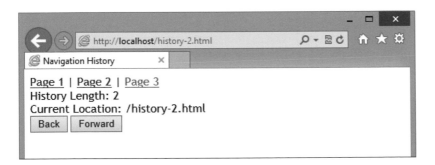

Hot tip

Remember that each URL only gets added to the history array when moving to a different page, not as each page gets loaded.

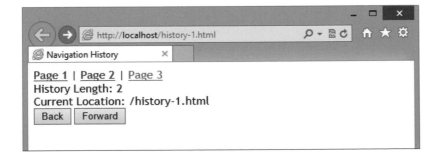

Summary

- The Document Object Model (DOM) is a hierarchical representation of all components of a web page

- The **window** object is the top level in the DOM hierarchy and has properties describing the browser window

- The **screen** object is a child of the **window** object and has properties describing the screen dimensions and color depth

- Dialog messages can be displayed using the window object's **alert()**, **confirm()**, and **prompt()** methods

- A popup window can be created using the window object's **open()** method but may be obstructed by a popup blocker

- The window object's **setTimeout()** method creates a timer, which can be canceled later using the **clearTimeout()** method

- The **navigator** object is a child of the **window** object and has properties describing the browser and host platform versions

- As the **window** object exists in the global namespace all its child objects need not include that part of the address, so that **window.navigator** can simply be referenced as **navigator**

- The practice of browser detection by querying the **navigator** properties is bad practice – feature detection should be used instead to ensure that DOM support exists

- The **navigator.plugins** and **navigator.mimeTypes** properties are both arrays on Mozilla browsers, in which each element contains details of a supported feature

- The **location** object is a child of the **window** object and has properties describing the address of the loaded document

- The **history** object is a child of the **window** object that contains an array of visited locations in the current session and has methods to navigate along its elements

8 Interacting with the document

This chapter demonstrates how to use properties and methods of the document object from the Document Object Model (DOM).

Extracting document info

Most interesting of all the DOM **window** object's children is the **document** object, which provides access to the HTML document. This has a number of properties describing the document and its location. The **document.title** property contains the value specified within the HTML document's title element.

The location of the HTML document is contained within the **document.URL** property, and is similar to the **location.href** value. The domain hosting the document is contained in the **document.domain** property, similar to the **location.host** value.

HTML documents supply the date of their creation or last modification as an HTTP header to the browser so it may decide whether to use a cached copy of the document or seek a new copy. This date can also be retrieved in JavaScript from the DOM's **document.lastModified** property.

Additionally, there is a **document.referrer** property that stores the URL of the web page containing the hyperlink that the user followed to load the current HTML document.

info-1.html

info-2.html

info.js

1 Create an HTML document that just contains a hyperlink to a second HTML document within its body section

```
<div>
<a href = "info-2.html" >Refer to the Next Page Here</a>
</div>
```

2 Now, create an HTML document that embeds an external script file and contains an element in which to write

```
<script type = "text/javascript" src = "info.js" > </script>
<div id = "panel" > </div>
```

3 Create the JavaScript file with an "init" function to initialize a variable when the document has loaded

```
function init()
{
  var panel = document.getElementById( "panel" ) ;
}
document.addEventListener( "DOMContentLoaded", init, false ) ;
```

4 Next, in the function block, insert statements to write properties of the current HTML document in the panel
```
panel.innerHTML += "Linked From: " + document.referrer ;
panel.innerHTML += "<br>Title: " + document.title ;
panel.innerHTML += "<br>URL: " + document.URL ;
panel.innerHTML += "<br>Domain: " + document.domain ;
panel.innerHTML +=
        "<br>Last Modified: " + document.lastModified ;
```

Don't forget

The date contained in **document.lastModified** relates to the HTML document, not style sheet or script files.

5 Save the script alongside the HTML document then open the first page in your browser to see the hyperlink

6 Now, click on the hyperlink to load the second HTML document in the browser and see document properties

Addressing component arrays

The DOM **document** object has child objects of **forms, anchors, images**, and **links**. Each of these children is an array in which every array element represents a document component in the same order they appear within the HTML document. For example, the first image in the document body, specified by an HTML **<img>** tag, is represented by **document.images[0]**. This means its URL can be referenced using **document.images[0].src**, which reveals the path assigned to the **src** attribute of the HTML **<img>** tag. Assigning this component a new URL in a script will dynamically replace the old image with a different image.

The anchors and links arrays both represent HTML **<a>** tags within the HTML document. Those tags that contain an **href** attribute appear as elements of the **links** array while those without an **href** attribute appear as elements within the **anchors** array.

Unsurprisingly, the **forms** array represents HTML **<form>** tags but also has its own child **elements** object that is an array of all the form components. For example, the value of the first component of the first form in an HTML document can be referenced using **document.forms[0].elements[0].value**. Assigning this component a new value in a script will dynamically replace the old value.

Don't forget

If the form and its components each have a name, subscript notation (described on page 96) can also be used. For example, **document.forms["f1"]. elements["el1"].value**.

components.html

1 Create an HTML document that embeds an external script file and contains an element in which to write
<script type = "text/javascript" src = "components.js" > </script><div id = "panel" > </div>

2 At the start of the body section of the HTML document, insert a form containing various components
**<form name = "f1"
        action = "processform.cgi" method = "GET" >
<div style = "width:450px ;background:url(bg.png);" >
<a name = "topOfForm" ></a>
<img src = "debate.png"
        alt = "Debate" height = "64"   width = "64" >
<input type = "text" name = "topic" size = "30" >
<input type = "button" value = "Ask a Question" >
<a href = "formhelp.html" >Need Help?</a>
<a name = "btmOfForm" ></a>
</div>
</form>**

debate.png   bg.png

3 Create the JavaScript file with an "init" function to initialize a variable as a reference to the panel

function init()
{
 var panel = document.getElementById("panel") ;
}
document.addEventListener("DOMContentLoaded", init, false) ;

components.js

4 Next, in the function block, insert statements to write the size of each component array and the URL of the first image

panel.innerHTML = "Document Components..." ;
panel.innerHTML +=
 **"
No. Forms: "+ document.forms.length ;**
panel.innerHTML +=
 **"
No. Links: " + document.links.length ;**
panel.innerHTML +=
 **"
No. Anchors: " + document.anchors.length ;**
panel.innerHTML +=
 **"
No. Images: " + document.images.length ;**
panel.innerHTML +=
 **"
First Image URL: "+ document.images[0].src ;**

5 Save the script alongside the HTML document then open the page in your browser to see the component arrays

Beware

Images that are incorporated within a document by style rules are not part of the images array, only those incorporated by HTML **<img>** tags – so here the **bg.png** form background image does not appear in the images array.

Addressing components direct

The technique of addressing components of an HTML document via the DOM component arrays, as described in the previous example, was for many years the only way to reference specific components in script, but has some serious limitations.

Firstly, using the component arrays with dot syntax requires the script author to count the number of components to calculate each index position. This is especially tedious with lengthy documents containing several forms and is error-prone. More seriously, modification of an HTML document, even in a modest way, could require the calculated component array index values to be modified to correctly reflect the new arrangement.

An alternative using subscript notation, where the HTML author names each component, allows the script author to reference components via their named DOM level. This allows the document to be modified providing no changes are made to the previously-named components, and all additional components are fastidiously named to allow the script author to continue to reference each component via their named DOM level.

This less than satisfactory situation was eventually resolved by the addition of two new methods to the **document** object:

● The **document.getElementById() method**, used throughout the examples in this book to reference the **<div>** element in the "JavaScript Console Panel", allows any component to be referenced by its HTML **id** attribute value. This method simply specifies the target **id** value as its string argument and is used to reference a single specific HTML element.

● The **document.getElementsByTagName()** method returns an array of all components in the document of the element name specified as its string argument. A specific HTML element can then be referenced using its array element index number.

While the **document.getElementsByTagName()** method is a useful addition it is the **document.getElementById()** method that is the true hero of the modern DOM as its introduction allows a specific HTML element to be referenced without knowledge of its hierarchical DOM address.

Beware

Scripts using the **getElementsByTagName()** method can still be adversely affected when the HTML document is modified but those using the heroic **getElementById()** method cannot.

1 Create an HTML document that embeds an external script file, contains lists, and has an element in which to write from JavaScript

```
<script type = "text/javascript" src = "direct.js"></script>
<ol><li>Alpha<li id = "item1" >Beta<li>Gamma</ol>
<ol><li>Delta<li>Epsilon<li>Zeta</ol>
<div id = "panel" > </div>
```

direct.html

2 Create the JavaScript file with an "init" function to initialize four variables by directly referencing document components

```
function init()
{
  var panel = document.getElementById( "panel" ) ;
  var item1 = document.getElementById( "item1" ) ;
  var elems = document.getElementsByTagName( "li" ) ;
  var item2 = elems[ 4 ] ;
}
document.addEventListener( "DOMContentLoaded", init, false ) ;
```

direct.js

3 Next, in the function block, insert statements to write the number of spans and two specific item values in the panel

```
panel.innerHTML += "Total No. List Items: " + elems.length ;
panel.innerHTML +=
        "<br>Specific Item One: " + item1.innerHTML +
        "<br>Specific Item Two: " + item2.innerHTML ;
```

4 Save the script alongside the HTML document then open the page in your browser to see the specific components

Don't forget

Notice that the only list item given an identity is the one to be targeted by **getElementById()**.

Setting and retrieving cookies

For security reasons JavaScript cannot write regular files on the user's hard drive, but it can write "cookie" files to store a small amount of data. These are limited in size to a maximum of 4 KB and in number to 20 per web server. Typically, the data stored in a cookie will identify the user for subsequent visits to a website.

Cookie data is stored in the DOM **document** object's **cookie** property as one or more "name=value" pairs, in which the values may not contain any whitespace, commas, or semi-colon characters. This requirement can be overcome, however, by passing the value as the argument to the built-in **escape()** method, which encodes the string in Unicode format. For example, this represents a space character as **%20**.

By default, the lifespan of a cookie is limited to the current browser session unless an expiry date is specified when the cookie is created as an "expires=date" pair, in which the date value is a GMT string. Typically this is achieved using a JavaScript **Date** object converted with its **toGMTString()** method.

Retrieving data from a cookie requires some string manipulation to return Unicode to regular text, using the **unescape()** method so **%20** becomes a space character once more, and to separate the name and value items of data. Within the cookie string the name and value appear either side of an "=" character, so this can be specified as the argument to the **split()** method to separate them. Similarly, where the value is a comma-separated list of items, the comma can be specified as the argument to the **split()** method to separate them as array elements.

Beware

The cookie expiry date cannot normally be read by JavaScript. If it is required to be readable also add it to the list of cookie values.

cookie.html

cookie.js

1 Create an HTML document that embeds an external script file and contains an element in which to write
<script type = "text/javascript" src = "cookie.js" > </script> <div id = "panel" > </div>

2 Create the JavaScript file with an "init" function to initialize a variable when the document has loaded
function init()
{
** var panel = document.getElementById("panel") ;**
}
document.addEventListener("DOMContentLoaded", init, false) ;

3 Next, in the function block, create an escaped value
and an expiry date then assign them to a cookie named
"myData"

```
var user = escape( "Mike McGrath,000456" ) ;
var expiry = new Date() ;
expiry.setTime( expiry.getTime() + ( 7*24*60*60*1000 ) ) ;
document.cookie = "myData=" + user + ";"
        + "expires=" + expiry.toGMTString() + ";" ;
```

4 Now, in the function block, unescape the cookie and
separate its value string

```
if ( document.cookie )
{
  var cookieString = unescape( document.cookie ) ;
  var list = cookieString.split( "=" ) ;
  if ( list[ 0 ] === "myData" )
  {
    var data = list[ 1 ].split( "," ) ;
    var userName = data[ 0 ] ;
    var userAcct = data[ 1 ] ;
  }
}
```

5 Finally, in the function block, insert statements to write
the cookie values in the panel

```
panel.innerHTML += "Cookie String: " + cookieString ;
panel.innerHTML += "<br>Split List: " + list ;
panel.innerHTML += "<br>User Name: " + userName ;
panel.innerHTML += "<br>User Account: " + userAcct ;
```

6 Save the script alongside the HTML document then open
the page in a browser to see the retrieved cookie values

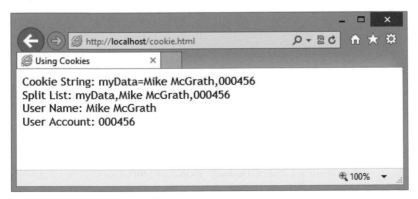

Writing with JavaScript

As witnessed in previous examples the **innerHTML** property of a document object can be assigned plain text, HTML elements, and other content to dynamically alter the document. Unusually, this process employs the browser's HTML parser, rather than the JavaScript engine, to insert the additional content and update the DOM tree. Although undocumented, the **innerHTML** property is a fast and effective way to write document content from JavaScript.

Additional content can be appended to the end of an HTML document by assignation to the **innerHTML** property of the **document.body** object, which represents the HTML **<body>** element. The appended content then appears after any other content in the browser window.

The DOM **document** object also has a **write()** method that provides another way to write content from JavaScript. When this method is called it automatically calls a **document.open()** method to start a new document – so content in the current document is no longer displayed. The content to be written is specified as the argument to the **document.write()** method and may include HTML elements, plain text, and other content. In order to write the content, internally the browser opens a "stream" which should always be closed after the content has been written by calling the **document.close()** method.

The **document.write()** method is sometimes seen in HTML script elements within the document body where it is called to write content when the document first loads in the browser. This is not in the spirit of unobtrusive JavaScript practice, as described on page 16, and should be avoided.

A script can dynamically write content to other windows it has opened by appending the **document.write()** method to that window object using dot syntax. This means that a script can create a popup window and dynamically write that window's content instead of loading an existing HTML document.

Beware

Do not confuse the **window.close()** method, which closes a window, with the **document.close()** method, which closes a writing stream.

1 Create an HTML document that embeds an external script file and has an element in which to write
<script type = "text/javascript" src = "write.js" ></script>
<div id = "panel" > </div>

write.html

write.js

2 Create the JavaScript file with an "init" function to initialize a variable and write the document's title in the panel
```
function init()
{
  var panel = document.getElementById( "panel" ) ;
  panel.innerHTML += document.title ;
}
document.addEventListener( "DOMContentLoaded", init, false ) ;
```

3 Next, in the function block, insert a statement to create a popup window
```
var pop =
open( "" , "" , "top=200,left=100,width=450,height=100" ) ;
```

4 Now, in the function block, insert statements to dynamically write content in the popup window
```
pop.document.write( "<title>Popup Window</title>" ) ;
pop.document.write( "<img src='debate.png'>" ) ;
pop.document.write( "Dynamic Popup Content" ) ;
pop.document.close() ;
```

5 Save the script alongside the HTML document then open the page in your browser to see the dynamically-written content

137

Don't forget

The arguments specifying URL and window name must be specified as empty strings when not required – see page 114 for more on popup windows.

Summary

- The **document** object is a child of the top-level **window** object and has properties describing the HTML document

- When the HTML document has been reached by the user following a hyperlink, the URL of the page containing the link is available in the **document.referrer** property

- The value specified by the HTML **<title>** element is also available from the **document.title** property

- The current location can be found in the **document.URL** property and the domain in the **document.domain** property

- In the DOM the **document** object has **forms**, **anchors**, **images**, and **links** component arrays

- A **document.forms** array has its own child **elements** array that can be used to reference a form's components

- The **document.getElementById()** method accepts an **id** of an HTML element attribute to reference that element without regard to the DOM hierarchy

- An array of all HTML elements of a specified tagname is returned by the **document.getElementsByTagName()** method

- Cookies store up to 4 KB of data on the user's computer and may optionally specify an expiry date

- Cookie data is stored as name=value pairs and the **escape()** method should be used to convert whitespace, commas, and semi-colons to Unicode format

- Retrieved cookie data can be converted from Unicode by the **unescape()** method and separated by the string **split()** method

- Changes to the **innerHTML** property of a document object are processed by the HTML parser and the DOM tree is updated

- Calling **document.write()** after the HTML document has loaded opens a new document in which to write content

9 Responding to actions

This chapter demonstrates how to create event-handler functions to respond to events that occur in the browser interface.

Reacting to window events

Examples in this book call an "init" function after the HTML document has loaded in the browser, at which time a "load event" occurs. The "event-handler" function is nominated by an assignation to the **window** object's **onload** property.

The browser fires other window "events" too, which can each be assigned a particular event-handler function. For example, when the user navigates to another web page, or closes the browser, an "unload event" occurs that can execute an event-handler function, which has been nominated by an assignation to the **window** object's **onunload** property.

Similarly, when a runtime error occurs the browser fires an "error event" for which an event-handler function can be nominated by assignation to the **window** object's **onerror** property. This event usefully passes three arguments to the nominated function describing the nature of the error, the URL of the file containing the error, and the line number in that file at which the error occurs. This means that the event-handler function definition must specify three arguments to receive the passed values. Additionally, the browser expects that function to return a value advising the status of the error. Returning a **true** value indicates that the error has been dealt with and allows the browser to continue happily. If a script does nominate an **onerror** event-handler function it should appear at the very start of the script to instruct the browser how to handle errors before it encounters any other code, which may subsequently contain errors.

Don't forget

It is preferable to provide predictive error-handling with the try-catch statement, described on page 74, as that can determine the error type.

onerror.html

onerror.js

1 Create an HTML document that embeds an external script file and contains an element in which to write
```
<script type = "text/javascript" src = "onerror.js" >
</script>
<div id = "panel" > </div>
```

2 Create the JavaScript file with a nominated function to handle any runtime error events that may occur
```
function errorhandler( msg , url , ln )
{
  alert( "Error: " + msg +
        "\nIn File: " + url + "\nAt Line: " + ln ) ;
}
onerror = errorhandler ;
```

3 At the end of the error-handler function block, insert a statement to instruct the browser that an error has indeed been handled
return true ;

4 After nominating an event-handler for errors add an "init" function to initialize a variable after the HTML document loads
```
function init()
{
  var panel = document.getElementById( "panel" ) ;
  panel.innerHTML = "Handling an error..." ;
}
document.addEventListener( "DOMContentLoaded", init, false ) ;
```

5 Next, in the init function block, insert a statement that erroneously attempts to reference an object that does not exist
document.getElementById("btn").value = "myButton" ;

6 Save the script alongside the HTML document then open the page in your browser to see the error handled

Hot tip

The **\n** escape sequence is used to specify a newline character in the alert dialog text.

Hot tip

The window object also has an onresize property to nominate an event-handler for when the window gets resized, and an onabort property to nominate an event-handler for when the user interrupts the loading of an image.

Responding to button clicks

Event-handler functions that execute when the user clicks on a particular object in the HTML document can be nominated by assignation to the object's **onclick** and **ondblclick** properties. These respond to the "click event" that fires, when the user clicks the mouse button once, and the "double-click event" that fires when the mouse button is pressed twice in quick succession.

Additionally an object's **onmousedown** and **onmouseup** properties can nominate event-handler functions to execute when the mouse button gets pressed down, firing the "mousedown event" and when it gets released, firing the "mouseup event".

As each event-handler function is then attached to a particular object it can simply reference the object to which it is attached using the JavaScript **this** keyword.

onclick.html

onclick.js

1. Create an HTML document that embeds an external script file and contains an element in which to write
```
<script type = "text/javascript" src = "onclick.js" >
</script>
<div id = "panel"> </div>
```

2. Create the JavaScript file with an "init" function to initialize a variable and write a phrase in the panel
```
function init()
{
  var panel = document.getElementById( "panel" ) ;
  panel.innerHTML = "Click Here &gt;<br>" ;
}
document.addEventListener( "DOMContentLoaded", init, false ) ;
```

3. Next, in the init function block, insert statements to attach event-handler functions to the panel object
```
panel.onclick = clickResponse ;
panel.ondblclick = dblclickResponse ;
panel.onmouseup = mouseupResponse ;
panel.onmousedown = mousedownResponse ;
```

4 Above the init function, insert the event-handler function definitions to respond to mouse button clicks

```
function clickResponse()
{ this.innerHTML += "Click detected<hr>" ; }

function dblclickResponse()
{ this.innerHTML += "Doubleclick detected<br>" ; }

function mousedownResponse()
{ this.innerHTML += "Mouse button down<br>" ; }

function mouseupResponse()
{ this.innerHTML += "Mouse button up<br>" ; }
```

Beware

If removing an object that has event-handlers attached it is important to also remove the event-handlers to avoid creating memory leaks.

5 Save the script alongside the HTML document then open the page in your browser and click an empty area of the panel to see the responses to the mouse button events

6 Now, refresh the browser to clear the click event responses, then double-click an empty area of the panel to see more responses

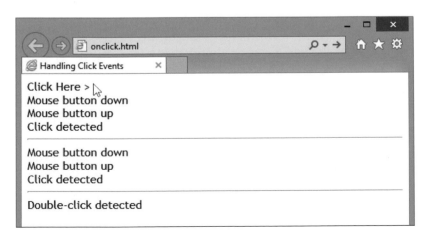

Acknowledging key strokes

Event-handler functions that execute when the user presses a keyboard key can be nominated by assignation to the **document** object's **onkeydown**, **onkeypress**, and **onkeyup** properties. These respond to the "keydown event" that fires when the user first presses a key, the "keypress event" that fires when the key is pressed down, and the "keyup event" that fires when the key is released.

Sadly, Internet Explorer's Document Object Model (DOM) and that of Mozilla-based browsers like Firefox, provide different solutions for handling keyboard events. Internet Explorer's **window** object provides an **event** child object that has a **keyCode** property, which stores the numerical value of the last key pressed. Other browsers pass a KeyboardEvent object as an argument to the event-handler function and that object has a **which** property containing the numerical value of the last key pressed. This means that a script must test for feature support to determine how to retrieve the numerical key value of the last key pressed.

The numerical value of a key is its Unicode value, which can be specified as the argument to the **String.fromCharCode()** method to translate it to a character value.

Hot tip

Unicode values for common characters are the same as ASCII code values, where lowercase a-z is 65-90 and A-Z is 97-122.

144

onkey.html

1   Create an HTML document that embeds an external script file and contains an element in which to write
```
<script type = "text/javascript" src = "onkey.js" >
</script>
<div id = "panel" > </div>
```

onkey.js

2   Create the JavaScript file and declare a global variable
```
var panel ;
```

3   Add an "init" function to initialize the global variable and write a phrase in the panel
```
function init()
{
  panel = document.getElementById( "panel" ) ;
  panel.innerHTML = "Press a key...<br>" ;
}
document.addEventListener( "DOMContentLoaded", init, false ) ;
```

4 Next, in the init function block, insert statements to attach event-handler functions to the document object
```
document.onkeydown = keydownResponse ;
document.onkeyup = keyupResponse ;
document.onkeypress = keypressResponse ;
```

5 Above the init function, insert the event-handler function definitions to respond to key presses
```
function keydownResponse()
{ panel.innerHTML += "<br>Key Pressed: " ; }

function keyupResponse()
{ panel.innerHTML += "<br>Key Released" ; }

function keypressResponse( e )
{
var keynum = ( window.event ) ? event.keyCode : e.which ;
panel.innerHTML += String.fromCharCode( keynum ) ;
}
```

6 Save the script alongside the HTML document then open the page in your browser and press some keys to see the responses

Beware

The **window** prefix is always required when testing for the presence of the **event** object as the evaluation is asking the question "does the **window** object have a child named **event** ?".

Recognizing mouse moves

Event-handler functions that execute when the user moves the mouse can be nominated by assignment to **onmousemove**, **onmouseover**, and **onmouseout** properties. These respond to the "mousemove event" that fires when the user moves the mouse in any direction, the "mouseover event" that fires when the pointer moves over the object to which the event is attached, and the "mouseout event" that fires when pointer moves off that object.

As with keyboard events, Internet Explorer's DOM and that of other browsers provide different solutions for handling mouse movement events. Internet Explorer's **window** object provides an **event** child object that has **x** and **y** properties, which store the current screen coordinates of the pointer. Other browsers pass a MouseEvent object as an argument to the event-handler function and that object has **pageX** and **pageY** properties containing the current pointer coordinates. This means that a script must test for feature support to determine how to retrieve the coordinates.

The event-handler function assigned to an object's **onmouseover** property can set a value when the pointer gets placed over that object, and the event-handler assigned to its **onmouseout** property can change the value when the pointer gets moved off that object.

onmouse.html

onmouse.js

1 Create an HTML document that embeds an external script file and contains a colored element in which to write
```
<script type = "text/javascript" src = "onmouse.js" >
</script>
<div id = "panel" style = "background:yellow" > </div>
```

2 Create the JavaScript file and declare two global variables
```
var panel , flag ;
```

3 Add an "init" function to initialize the global variables and write a phrase in the panel
```
function init()
{
  panel = document.getElementById( "panel" ) ;
  flag = true ;
  panel.innerHTML = "Move the mouse..." ;
}
document.addEventListener( "DOMContentLoaded", init, false ) ;
```

4 Next, in the init function block, insert statements to attach event-handlers to the document and to the panel object

```
document.onmousemove = mousemoveResponse ;
panel.onmouseover = mouseoverResponse ;
panel.onmouseout = mouseoutResponse ;
```

Don't forget

In this example the pointer coordinates are dynamically displayed in the panel unless the pointer is actually over the panel object.

5 Above the init function, insert the event-handler function definitions to respond to mouse movements

```
function mousemoveResponse( e )
{
  var x , y ;

  if ( window.event ) { x = event.x ; y = event.y ; }
  else if( e ) { x = e.pageX ; y = e.pageY ; }

  if ( flag )
  { panel.innerHTML = "Mouse is at X: " + x + ", Y: " + y ; }
}

function mouseoverResponse()
{ flag = false ; panel.innerHTML = "Mouse is Over" ; }

function mouseoutResponse() { flag = true ; }
```

6 Save the script alongside the HTML document then open the page in your browser and move the mouse to see the responses

Identifying focus

Event-handler functions that execute when the user moves focus from one document object to another can be nominated by assignation to **onfocus** and **onblur** properties. These respond to the "focus event" that fires when the object receives focus, and the "blur event" that fires when the object loses focus. Typically these are used on form text input fields where the user can tab from one field to the next, giving focus to each current field in turn. Also, the user can click the pointer on any field to give it focus – indicated by the appearance of a flashing cursor, ready to receive input. Additionally, JavaScript can call the field's **focus()** method to give it focus.

onfocus.html

onfocus.js

Create an HTML document that embeds an external script file and contains an element in which to write
```
<script type = "text/javascript" src = "onfocus.js" >
</script>
<div id = "panel" > </div>
```

Create the JavaScript file with an "init" function to initialize a variable and write two HTML text input elements in the panel
```
function init()
{
  var panel = document.getElementById( "panel" ) ;
  panel.innerHTML += "<input type = 'text' id = 'txt1'>" ;
  panel.innerHTML += "<input type = 'text' id = 'txt2'>" ;
}
document.addEventListener( "DOMContentLoaded", init, false ) ;
```

Next, in the function block, insert statements to nominate event-handler functions for the focus and blur events of each text input
```
var field1 = document.getElementById( "txt1" ) ;
field1.onfocus = focusResponse ;
field1.onblur = blurResponse ;

var field2 = document.getElementById( "txt2" ) ;
field2.onfocus = focusResponse ;
field2.onblur = blurResponse ;
```

Now, in the function block, add a statement to set the focus in the first text input field when the page loads
```
field1.focus() ;
```

5 Above the init function, insert the event-handler function definitions to respond to receipt and loss of focus
function focusResponse()
{ this.value = "In Focus" ; }

function blurResponse()
{ this.value = "Focus Lost" ; }

Don't forget

The **this** keyword identifies which input field is calling the event-handler function and sets the value of that field.

6 Save the script alongside the HTML document then open the page in your browser and see the first text field receive focus

7 Now, click on the second text field to give it focus and see focus blur from the first text field

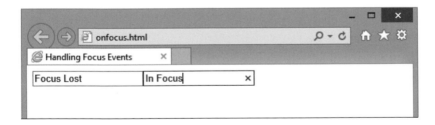

8 Finally, click on the document outside the panel to move focus from the second text field

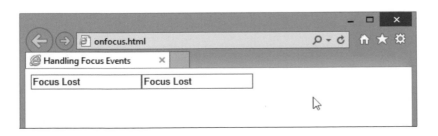

Summary

- An event-handler function for a window event is nominated by assigning the function name to a **window** object property

- When the browser fires an event it seeks an event-handler for that event and, if one exists, will execute its statements

- The load event is fired when the window has loaded a document and its event-handler is sought via the **window** object's **onload** property

- The unload event is fired when the user navigates to a new location, or closes the browser, and its event-handler is sought via the **window** object's **onunload** property

- A runtime error event passes three arguments to the event-handler nominated by the **window** object's **onerror** property describing the nature and script location of the error

- Mouse button click events seek event-handlers via the clicked object's **onclick** and **ondblclick** properties, and also its **onmousedown** and **onmouseup** properties

- Internet Explorer provides a **window.event** object that has **event.keyCode**, **event.x** and **event.y** properties storing key values and coordinates

- Mozilla browsers pass KeyboardEvent and MouseEvent objects as arguments to the event-handler that have **which**, **pageX** and **pageY** properties storing key values and coordinates

- Key stroke events can seek event-handlers via the **document** object's **onkeydown, onkeypress,** and **onkeyup** properties

- Mouse movement events can seek event-handlers via the **onmousemove, onmouseover,** and **onmouseout** properties of the object over which the pointer is moving

- Focus events can seek event-handlers via an object's **onfocus** and **onblur** properties, and a statement can ensure an object receives the focus by calling that object's **focus()** method

10 Processing HTML forms

This chapter demonstrates how to examine user input form values and implement validation before submission to the web server.

Assigning values

Each element of a form can be dynamically assigned values from a script. A reference to the element can be gained using the **document.getElementById()** method, if it contains an id attribute, or hierarchically using the **document.forms[].elements[]** component arrays. Each attribute can then be assigned a value by suffixing the attribute name to the reference using dot syntax.

assign.html

1 Create an HTML document that embeds an external script file and contains a form with two text inputs and a submit button
```
<script type = "text/javascript" src = "assign.js"></script>
<form id = "book" >
  <div id = "panel" >
    <input id = "title" type = "text" > <br>
    <input id = "author" type = "text" >
    <input type = "submit" value = "Submit" >
  </div>
</form>
```

assign.js

2 Create the JavaScript file with an "init" function to initialize a variable and add a phrase in the panel
```
function init()
{
  var panel = document.getElementById( "panel" ) ;
  panel.innerHTML + = "Send Book Data" ;
}
document.addEventListener( "DOMContentLoaded", init, false ) ;
```

Hot tip

Refer back to page 130 for more on DOM component arrays.

3 Next, in the init function block, insert statements to specify a submission method and a server-side script to process the form
```
var form = document.getElementById( "book" ) ;
form.action = "echo.pl" ;
form.method = "POST" ;
```

4 Now, in the function block, insert statements to assign values to the first text input field
```
var title = document.getElementById( "title" ) ;
title.size = "30" ;
title.name = "Book Title" ;
title.value = "JavaScript in easy steps" ;
```

5 Finally, in the function block, insert statements to assign values to the second text input field
**var author = document.getElementById("author") ;
author.size = "30" ;
author.name = "By Author" ;
author.value = "Mike McGrath" ;**

Don't forget

This script is submitted via HTTP to a web server that contains the **echo.pl** server-side PERL script to process the submitted form values.

6 Save the script alongside the HTML document then open the page in your browser to see the assigned form values

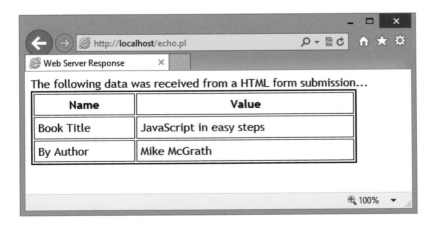

153

7 Click the submit button to see the server-side script response echo the submitted name=value pairs assigned by the script

Name	Value
Book Title	JavaScript in easy steps
By Author	Mike McGrath

Polling radios & checkboxes

Radio button groups allow the user to select any one button from the group. All radio button input elements in that group must share the same HTML 'name' attributes value. In scripting terms that group name is the name of an array in which each radio button object can be referenced using its array index value.

Unlike radio button groups, checkbox button groups allow the user to select one or more buttons in that group. But as with radio button groups each name attribute shares the same group name. That group name is also the name of an array in which each checkbox button object can be referenced by its array index value.

Both radio button objects and checkbox button objects have a **checked** boolean property, which is **true** when the button is selected and **false** otherwise. Looping through a button group array to inspect the checked property of each object determines which buttons are selected. A script statement can also assign a **true** value to the checked property of a button to select it.

Hot tip

When multiple buttons in a checkbox button group have been selected, their values are submitted as a comma-separated list.

poll.html

1 Create an HTML document that embeds an external script file and contains a form with two button groups and a button

```
<script type = "text/javascript" src = "poll.js" ></script>
<form id = "pizza" action = "echo.pl" method = "POST">
  <div id = "panel" > Pizza Topping?
    <input type = "checkbox"
        name = "Topping" value = "Cheese" >Cheese
    <input type = "checkbox"
        name = "Topping" value = "Ham" >Ham
  <input type = "checkbox"
        name = "Topping" value = "Peppers" >Peppers
    <input type = "button"
        id = "btn" value = "Confirm Choices" >
  </div>
</form>
```

poll.js

2 Create the JavaScript file with an "init" function to check the first button in the group and nominate a button click event-handler

```
function init()
{
document.getElementById( "pizza" ).Topping[0]checked = true;
document.getElementById( "btn" ).onclick = poll ;
}
document.addEventListener( "DOMContentLoaded", init, false ) ;
```

3 Above the init function block, insert the event-handler function to confirm the selected buttons and send the form

```
function poll()
{
  var i , isOk , summary = "" ;
  var form = document.getElementById( "pizza" ) ;

  for ( i = 0 ; i < form.Topping.length ; i++ )
  {
    if ( form.Topping[ i ].checked )
    { summary += form.Topping[ i ].value + " " ; }
  }
  isOk = confirm( "Submit these choices?\n" + summary ) ;
  if ( isOk ){ form.submit() ; } else { return false ; }
}
```

Hot tip

Notice how the form's **submit()** method is used here to send the form rather than an HTML submit button.

4 Save the script alongside the HTML document then open the page in your browser, choose a second checkbox button from the group then click the push button

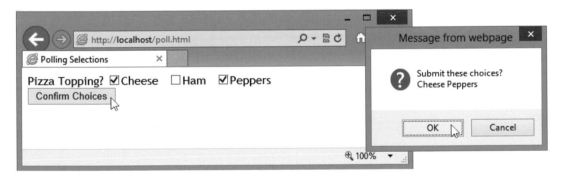

5 Click the OK button to confirm your choices and to submit the form data

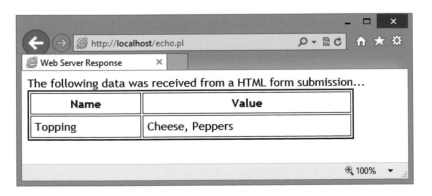

Choosing options

Options presented in an HTML **<select>** list object are uniquely represented in the DOM by an **options[]** array, in which each array element contains the option specified by an HTML **<option>** tag. Upon submission to the web server the value assigned to the **name** attribute of the **<select>** tag, and that assigned to the **value** attribute of the currently selected **<option>** tag, are sent as a name=value pair.

Importantly, the selection list object has a **selectedIndex** property, which contains the index number of the currently-selected **options[]** array element, and this can be used to retrieve the value of the current selected option.

select.html

1 Create an HTML document that embeds an external script file and contains a form with a selection list and a submit button

```
<script type = "text/javascript" src = "select.js"></script>
<form action = "echo.pl" method = "POST" >
<div id = "panel" >
<select id = "cityList" name = "City" >
  <option value = "London" >London</option>
  <option value = "New York" selected>New York</option>
  <option value = "Paris" >Paris</option>
  <option value = "Dubai" >Dubai</option>
  <option value = "Sydney" >Sydney</option>
</select>
<input type = "submit" >
</div>
</form>
```

select.js

2 Create the JavaScript file with an "init" function to initialize two variables when the document has loaded

```
function init()
{
  var panel = document.getElementById( "panel" ) ;
  var list = document.getElementById( "cityList" ) ;
}
document.addEventListener( "DOMContentLoaded", init, false ) ;
```

3 Next, in the function block, write the index number and the value of the currently-selected option in the panel

```
var elem = list.options.selectedIndex ;
var city = list.options[ elem ].value ;
panel.innerHTML +=
        "Selected: " + city + " - Index: " + elem ;
```

4 Save the script alongside the HTML document then open the web page in your browser to see the current selection

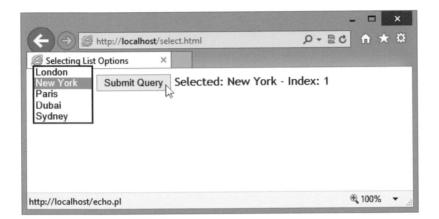

5 Submit the form to see the name of the selection list and the value of the current selection sent as a name=value pair

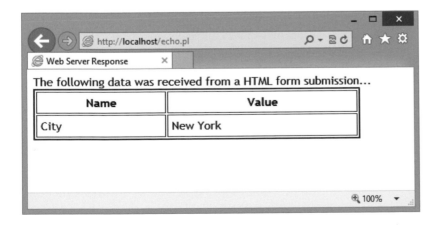

The following data was received from a HTML form submission...

Name	Value
City	New York

Don't forget

Notice that the HTML **selected** attribute selects the second option element, which is represented in the DOM by **options[1]**.

Hot tip

Hierarchically this selected option can be referenced using **document.forms[0]. elements[0].options[1]. value** – the deepest level of the DOM.

157

Reacting to form changes

An event-handler can be nominated to the **onchange** property of form text input objects and textarea objects to respond to changes in their content. Interestingly, the change event is not fired until the text element loses focus, at which point the new content of the text field becomes the value of that form element. This is preferable to firing a change event each time a character gets added to the text field.

Usefully, an event-handler can be nominated to the **onreset** property of a form object to remove content related to form input when the form is returned to its original state by a reset button.

change.html

1 Create an HTML document that embeds an external script file and contains a form with a text input and a reset button, followed by an element in which to write

```
<script type = "text/javascript" src = "change.js"></script>
<form id = "lang" action = "echo.pl" method = "POST" >
  <input id = "txt" type = "text" size = "30"
                                 value = "JavaScript" >
  <input type = "reset" >
</form>
<div id = "panel"> </div>
```

change.js

2 Create the JavaScript file by declaring three global variables

```
var panel , field , saved ;
```

3 After the variable declaration, add an "init" function to initialize each global variable plus one local variable

```
function init()
{
  panel = document.getElementById( "panel" ) ;
  field = document.getElementById( "txt" ) ;
  saved = field.value ;
  var form = document.getElementById( "lang" ) ;
}
document.addEventListener( "DOMContentLoaded", init, false ) ;
```

4 Next, in the function block, attach event-handler functions to the form object and text field object, then call a function

```
form.onreset = wipe ;
field.onchange = update ;
wipe() ;
```

5   Above the init function, insert the event-handler function definitions to respond to text field changes, window load, and form reset events

function update()
{
  panel.innerHTML =
          saved + " changed to " + field.value + "<br>" ;
  saved = field.value ;
}

function wipe() { panel.innerHTML = "<br>" ; }

Hot tip

The change event of a selection list fires instantly when the user selects a different list item.

6   Save the script alongside the HTML document then open the web page in your browser to see the initial text field value

159

7   Now, modify the content in the text field then click on the page so the text field loses focus to see the changes

8   Finally, click the reset button to resume the original state

Beware

Text fields also have an **onselect** property to which an event-handler can be nominated to respond when the user selects some of its text. Implementation of the select event in text fields can be problematic however, so this property is best avoided.

Submitting valid forms

A form object's **onsubmit** property can nominate an event-handler function to validate the user input entered into a form before it is submitted to the web server for processing. By default, that function will return a **true** value upon completion but when it returns a **false** value the form will not be submitted.

The simplest level of form validation examines a text input where an entry is required to ensure the user has made an entry. When its value remains an empty string, no entry has been made so the validating function can return **false** to prevent form submission.

A higher level of form validation can examine the string entered by the user to ensure it meets an expected format. For example, where an email address is expected, the format requires the string to contain an "@" character and at least one "." character. When either of these are absent the string is not a valid email address so the validating function can return **false** to prevent form submission.

validate.html

1 Create an HTML document that embeds an external script file and contains a form with two text inputs and a submit button, followed by an element in which to write
```
<script type = "text/javascript" src = "validate.js" >
</script>
<form id = "contact" action = "echo.pl" method = "POST">
Name: <input type = "text" size = "30" name = "Name">
<br>
Email : <input type = "text" size = "30" name = "Email">
<input type = "submit" >
</form>
<div id = "panel" > </div>
```

validate.js

2 Create the JavaScript file with an "init" function to initialize a variable and write a phrase in the panel
```
function init()
{
  var panel = document.getElementById( "panel" ) ;
  panel.innerHTML =
          "Please enter your name and email address." ;
}
document.addEventListener( "DOMContentLoaded", init, false ) ;
```

3 Next, in the function block, attach an event-handler function to the form object
```
var form = document.getElementById( "contact" ) ;
form.onsubmit = validate ;
```

4 Above the init function, insert the event-handler function definition to respond to the form submission request

```
function validate()
{
  if ( this.elements[ "Name" ].value === "" )
  { alert( "Please enter your name" ) ; return false ; }

  if ( ( this.elements[ "Email" ].value.indexOf( "@" ) === -1 )
  || ( this.elements[ "Email" ].value.indexOf( "." ) === -1 ) )
  { alert( "Please enter a valid email address" ) ; return false ; }
}
```

5 Save the script alongside the HTML document then open the web page in your browser and try to submit the form with invalid input

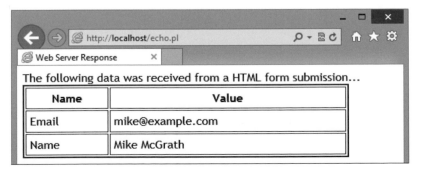

Summary

- Each element of a form can be dynamically assigned a value from JavaScript

- If a form element contains an id attribute, that element can be referenced using the **document.getElementById()** method

- A form element that does not contain an id attribute can be referenced using the **document.forms[].elements[]** arrays

- The value assigned to the **name** attribute of a radio button group or checkbox button group is also the name of an array in which each button can be referenced by their index value

- When a form radio button or checkbox button has been selected its **checked** property becomes a **true** value

- A loop can be used to examine the **checked** property of each button in a button group to determine which are selected

- The options of a selection list object are represented in the DOM by its **options[]** array

- A selection list object has a **selectedIndex** property containing the array element index value of the currently-selected option

- The value of the current selected option can be retrieved by specifying the **selectedIndex** value in the **options[]** array

- An event-handler function can be nominated by the **onchange** property to respond to changes in text field content

- An event-handler function can be nominated by the **onreset** property to respond when the user pushes a form's reset button

- An event-handler function can be nominated by the **onsubmit** property to respond when the user pushes a submit button

- When the **onsubmit** event-handler returns a **false** value the form will not be submitted

- A form can be submitted from script by calling the **submit()** method of the form object

11 Creating dynamic effects

This chapter demonstrates how to change page content in response to user actions to create dynamic effects.

Swapping backgrounds

The appearance of an object in an HTML document can be dynamically manipulated from JavaScript by assigning new values to its presentational DOM properties. These have similar names to CSS style sheet properties except hyphenated CSS property names adopt camel case for DOM property names. For example, the CSS **text-align** property is represented by the **textAlign** DOM property.

All the presentational DOM properties are contained within a parent **style** property, which is a child of the object. This means that a presentational property can be addressed using dot syntax, such as for an object named "obj" with **obj.style.textAlign**.

Assigning new values to an object background in response to the mouseover, mousedown, mouseup, and mouseout events creates the popular "rollover" effect.

rollover.html

rollover.js

1. Create an HTML document that embeds an external script file and contains a simple element
```
<script type = "text/javascript" src = "rollover.js" >
</script>
<div id = "active" >Button</div>
```

2. Create the JavaScript file with an "init" function that initializes a global variable as a reference to the div element
```
var obj ;

function init()
{
  obj = document.getElementById( "active" ) ;
}
document.addEventListener( "DOMContentLoaded", init, false ) ;
```

3. In the function block, insert statements to specify some presentational properties of the div element
```
obj.style.width = "100px" ;
obj.style.background = "aqua" ;
obj.style.padding = "5px" ;
obj.style.border = "2px solid black" ;
obj.style.textAlign = "center" ;
```

④ Next, in the function block, insert statements to attach event-handler functions to the div object
obj.onmouseover = over ;
obj.onmousedown = down ;
obj.onmouseup = up ;
obj.onmouseout = out ;

⑤ Above the init function, insert the event-handler function definitions to respond to mouse actions
function over() { obj.style.background = "yellow" ; }
function down() { obj.style.background = "lime" ; }
function up()   { obj.style.background = "yellow" ; }
function out()   { obj.style.background = "aqua" ; }

⑥ Save the script alongside the HTML document then open the web page in your browser and click the div element to see the rollover effect

Hot tip

The **style.background** property can also be assigned images in CSS format to create an image rollover effect. For example, **obj.style.background= "url(bg.png)"**.

Don't forget

Other differences between CSS and DOM presentational properties include **marginTop** for **margin-top**, **zIndex** for **z-index**, and **backgroundColor** for **background-color**.

165

Toggling visibility

The visibility of an object in an HTML document can be dynamically manipulated from JavaScript by toggling the value of its DOM **style.visibility** property from "hidden" to "visible", and back again. Absolutely positioning the object with CSS rules, or by specifying values to the equivalent DOM properties in script, can determine precisely where the object will appear when visible.

Assigning new values to an object's **style.visibility** property in response to the **mouseover** and **mouseout** events creates the "popup layer" effect, which is now often used instead of popup windows.

toggle.html

Don't forget

CSS rules are best listed in a separate file for ease of maintenance. Inline rules are only given in this example to save on page space.

 Create an HTML document that embeds an external script file
```
<script type = "text/javascript" src = "toggle.js"></script>
```

Create the JavaScript file with an "init" function that initializes a global variable as a reference to the second div element

In the body section of the document, add two elements with multiple style rules to position the elements precisely adjacent
```
<div id = "contentLayer"
style = "position : absolute ; top : 20px ; left : 20px ;
         width : 196px ; height : 46px ; padding : 5px ;
         border : 2px dashed red ;">
Permanent Original Content</div>

<div id = "popupLayer"
style = "position : absolute ; top : 20px ; left : 230px ;
         width : 200px ; height : 50px ; padding : 5px ;
         background : red ; color : white ;" >
Additional Popup Content</div>
```

Create the JavaScript file with an "init" function that initializes a global variable as a reference to the second div element
```
var pop ;

function init()
{
  pop = document.getElementById( "popupLayer" ) ;
}
document.addEventListener( "DOMContentLoaded", init, false ) ;
```

Insert a statement in the function block to hide the second div element when the document loads
```
pop.style.visibility = "hidden" ;
```

5 Next, in the function block, initialize a local variable as a reference to the first div element
var obj = document.getElementById("contentLayer") ;

6 Now, in the function block, insert statements to attach event-handlers to the first div element
obj.onmouseover = showPop ;
obj.onmouseout = hidePop ;

7 Above the init function, insert the event-handler function definitions
function showPop() { pop.style.visibility = "visible" ; }
function hidePop() { pop.style.visibility = "hidden" ; }

8 Save the script alongside the HTML document then open the web page in your browser and move the pointer over the visible element to see the other element appear and disappear

Beware

Avoid creating directly-adjacent elements that both respond to mouse events – leave a small gap to allow the **mouseout** event to fire before the next **mouseover** event fires.

Hot tip

You can assign different values to the **zIndex** property of overlapping elements to determine which should appear on top.

Rotating image source

Images in an HTML document can be dynamically exchanged from JavaScript by assigning a different image file URL to the image object's **src** attribute. Including this procedure in a function that is repeatedly called by a timer produces a "slideshow" effect.

All the images that are to appear in the slideshow can be loaded into the browser's cache by a preload routine that assigns each image URL to new Image objects. This ensures each image is available for instant display when it is needed to replace the previous image in the slideshow.

slideshow.html

slideshow.js

1 Create an HTML document that embeds an external script file
```
<script type = "text/javascript" src= "slideshow.js" ></script>
```

2 In the body section of the document, add an image element
```
<div>
<img id = "pic" width = "120" height = "120"
                        alt = "Icon" src = "query.png" >
</div>
```

3 Create the JavaScript file declaring three global variables to act as a counter, an array of image URLs, and a reference to the image element object
```
var i , imgs , pic ;
```

4 Add an "init" function that begins by getting a reference to the image element object
```
function init()
{
pic = document.getElementById( "pic" ) ;
}
document.addEventListener( "DOMContentLoaded", init, false ) ;
```

5 Next, in the function block, create an array of image file URLs
```
imgs =
[ "query.png" , "warn.png" , "stop.png" , "info.png" ] ;
```

6 Now, in the function block, insert a preload routine to load the image files into the browser's cache

```
var preload = new Array() ;
for ( i = 0 ; i < imgs.length ; i++ )
{
  preload[ i ] = new Image() ;
  preload[ i ].src = imgs[ i ] ;
}
```

Hot tip

Ensure all images are the actual size to be displayed so the browser need not resize them.

7 Finally, in the function block, reset the counter to zero then call a function to start the slideshow sequence

```
i = 0 ;
rotate() ;
```

8 Above the init function, insert the slideshow sequence function definition

```
function rotate()
{
  pic.src = imgs[ i ] ;                // Assign an image URL.
  // Then change the counter.
  ( i === ( imgs.length - 1 ) ) ? ( i = 0 ) : ( i++ ) ;
  setTimeout( rotate , 1000 ) ;
}
```

9 Save the script alongside the HTML document then open the web page in your browser to see the slideshow

Hot tip

Increase the timer interval from 1000 milliseconds to lengthen the interval between changes and simply add more image URLs to the array to extend the slideshow.

Enlarging thumbnails

A web page may contain a large number of small "thumbnail" images to provide a visual representation of a number of items. Their small image file sizes avoid the latency issues that could arise if larger, more detailed, images were used, yet JavaScript can supply individual "enlarged" images in response to user actions.

Enlarging a thumbnail image, so that it is displayed beyond its actual pixel dimensions, produces an unsatisfactory pixellated version. It is generally preferable to display the full-size image from which the thumbnail has been reduced. Naming the thumbnail images with the name of their full-size version plus an additional suffix allows easy reference of the large image by using string manipulation to remove the suffix from the thumbnail

zoom.html

1 Create an HTML document that embeds an external script file
```
<script type = "text/javascript" src = "zoom.js"></script>
```

2 In the body section of the document, add a div element containing thumbnail images and some text
```
<div style = "width:220px" >
<img id = "heli" src = "heli_thumb.png"
  alt = "Helicopter Image" width = "100" height = "58" >
<img id = "car" src = "car_thumb.png"
  alt = "Car Image" width = "100" height = "58" >
Place the pointer on either image to get a larger view.
</div>
```

3 Now, add a div element in which to display enlarged images
```
<div id = "zoomBox" style = "position : absolute ;
top : 10px ; left : 220px ; width : 300px ; height : 174px ;">
</div>
```

zoom.js

4 Create the JavaScript file with an "init" function that initializes a global variable as a reference to the second div element
```
var box ;

function init()
{
  box = document.getElementById( "zoomBox" ) ;
}
document.addEventListener( "DOMContentLoaded", init, false ) ;
```

5 In the function block, get references to each image object and attach event-handler functions to them
```
var heli = document.getElementById( "heli" ) ;
heli.onmouseover = zoomIn ;
heli.onmouseout = zoomOut ;

var car = document.getElementById( "car" ) ;
car.onmouseover = zoomIn ;
car.onmouseout = zoomOut ;
```

6 Above the init function, insert the event-handler function definitions
```
function zoomIn()
{
  var filename = this.src.split( "_thumb.png" ) ;
  box.style.background = "url(" + filename[ 0 ] + ".png)" ;
}

function zoomOut()
{
  box.style.background = "inherit" ;
}
```

7 Save the script alongside the HTML document then open the web page in your browser and place the pointer over a thumbnail to see its enlarged version

Hot tip

Here, the **split()** method stores the start of the path in the first array element to which the file extension gets concatenated.

Don't forget

The thumbnail images in this example have dimensions one third those of the larger versions, and filesizes around one eighth of the larger versions.

171

Animating elements

The position of an object in an HTML document can be dynamically manipulated from JavaScript by assigning new values to its presentational DOM properties. Incorporating this ability within a timer function creates an "animation" effect, in which the object is continuously repositioned in the document.

animate.html

1 Create an HTML document that embeds an external script file
```
<script type = "text/javascript" src = "animate.js" ></script>
```

2 In the body section of the document, add a div element with an image background
```
<div id = "boat" style = "width : 120px ; height : 105px ;
            background : url( sail_r.png )" > </div>
```

animate.js

3 Create the JavaScript file that declares three global variables and has an "init" function to preload a second image, which can be swapped later for the div background
```
var obj , w , goRight ;

function init()
{
  var preload = new Image() ;
  preload.src = "sail_l.png" ;
}
document.addEventListener( "DOMContentLoaded", init, false ) ;
```

Hot tip

An object's horizontal position can be manipulated by assigning new values to its **style.top** property.

4 Next, in the function block, initialize the three variables as a reference to the div object, the width of the browser window, and a boolean value to determine the direction of movement
```
obj = document.getElementById( "boat" ) ;
w = document.body.clientWidth ;
goRight = true ;
```

5 Now, in the function block, insert statements to specify the initial position of the div element
```
obj.style.position = "absolute" ;
obj.style.left = "-120px" ;
```

6 Finally, in the function block, call a function to animate the div
```
setSail() ;
```

7   Above the init function, begin the animating function by getting the div element's current position

```
function setSail()
{
  var pos = parseInt( obj.style.left , 10 ) ;
}
```

8   Next, in the animating function, increment or decrement the current position according to the direction of movement

```
( goRight ) ? pos++ : pos-- ;
obj.style.left = pos + "px" ;
```

9   Now, in the animating function, add statements to reverse the direction of movement and replace the background image when the element position exceeds the window edges

```
if ( pos > ( w + 40 ) )
{
  obj.style.background = "url( sail_l.png )" ;
  goRight = false ;
}

if ( pos < -140 )
{
  obj.style.background = "url( sail_r.png )" ;
  goRight = true ;
}
```

10   Finally, in the animating function, insert the recursive timer statement specifing the movement interval

```
setTimeout( setSail , 10 );
```

11   Save the script alongside the HTML document then open the web page in your browser to see the animated element

---

Hot tip

The **document.body** object has **clientWidth** and **clientHeight** properties containing the current browser window dimensions.

sail_r.png   sail_l.png

173

Don't forget

The position value has a "px" suffix, which must be removed before manipulation and added after manipulation.

Summary

- The appearance of an object in an HTML document can be dynamically manipulated from JavaScript by assigning new values to its presentational DOM properties

- All presentational DOM properties are contained within the **style** property, which is a child of the object

- A rollover effect can be created by assigning new values to an object's **style.background** property in response to **mouseover, mousedown, mouseup,** and **mouseout** events

- A popup layer effect can be created by toggling an object's **style.visibility** property between **hidden** and **visible** values

- Images that are to appear in a slideshow can be preloaded into the browser's cache so they are available when required

- A slideshow effect can be created by sequentially assigning the path to an image file to an image object's **src** property within a timer function

- The original full-size version of a thumbnail image can be downloaded in response to a user action

- The position of an object in an HTML document can be dynamically manipulated by assigning new values to its **style.left** and **style.top** DOM properties

- An animation effect can be created by assigning new position values within a timer function to continuously reposition an object on the page

- The **style.left** and **style.top** values have a "px" suffix that must be removed before manipulating the numerical value

- Current browser window size in pixels can be found in the **document.body.clientWidth** property

12 Producing web apps

This chapter demonstrates how to create rich internet applications that can seamlessly update page content from the web server.

Introducing AJAX

Several mature web technologies can be used in harmony to create web-based applications that have similar responsiveness to that of traditional desktop applications. A web-based application is sometimes referred to as a "Rich Internet Application" (RIA).

The combined techniques employed by a web-based application are known generically as "AJAX" (Asynchronous JavaScript And XML) and incorporates these features:

- Standards-based presentation – using HTML and CSS

- Dynamic display and interaction – using the DOM

- Data interchange and manipulation – using XML and text

- Asynchronous retrieval – using an **XMLHttpRequest** object

- JavaScript functionality – to control the whole process

AJAX is not a technology itself but simply describes a technique combining other technologies. To fully appreciate its advantages it is necessary to understand the relationship between the web browser and the web server.

Typically, a user action in the web browser will send a request to the web server via HyperText Transfer Protocol (HTTP). When the web server receives the request it processes it, by calling upon server-side scripts and databases as required, then sends a response back to the browser via HTTP. When the web browser receives the response it can then update its contents accordingly.

Don't forget

AJAX is simply a new approach to the use of existing technologies.

The round-trip time taken to receive a response to a web server request can be lengthy. This interval is known as "network latency" and it can try the user's patience.

A web-based application can overcome the need to wait for web server responses by introducing an AJAX "engine" to serve as an intermediary in the request-response cycle.

Beware

Alert, prompt, and confirm dialogs temporarily lock the browser thread until the user pushes one of their buttons. This also halts the AJAX engine so those dialogs should never be used with web-based applications.

The AJAX engine, written in JavaScript, gets loaded as the web page opens in the web browser so the user can instantly interact with the application. User actions that may previously have made a request to the web server can now take the form of a JavaScript call to the AJAX engine. Responses that do not require contact with the web server, such as data validation or editing data in memory, can be fulfilled internally by the AJAX engine. Other responses that do require contact with the web server, such as the submission of data for processing or retrieval of new data, are made asynchronously without interrupting the user's interaction with the application. In either case, the content displayed by the browser can be dynamically updated using the DOM **innerHTML** property when the response is received.

Sending an HTTP request

At the core of every AJAX engine is an **XMLHttpRequest** object that allows requests to be sent from JavaScript to the web server. An instance of this object is created with the **new** keyword and the request is specified as three arguments to its **open()** method stating the retrieval method, a URL, and a boolean **true** value to make the request asynchronously. The request can then be sent by calling the object's **send()** method, which requires a single argument specifying text to be sent to the server or the **null** keyword. Finally, an event-handler must be nominated to the **XMLHttpRequest** object's **onreadystatechange** property to handle the response from the web server.

At each stage of the request process the object's **readyState** property gets assigned a number:

0 – the request is unintialized, as **open()** has not been called
1 – the request is specified, but **send()** has not been called
2 – the request is being sent, as **send()** has now been called
3 – the response is being received, but is not yet complete
4 – the response is complete and returned data is available

Upon completion, when the **readyState** property has been set to 4, the **XMLHttpRequest** object's **status** property is assigned an HTTP status code describing the result of the request:

200 – OK, the request succeeded
401 – Unauthorized, authentication has not been provided
403 – Forbidden, the server is refusing to respond
404 – Not found, the requested resource is absent

The event-handler nominated to handle the response can first test that the **readyState** property is 4 and the status property is 200 to ensure that the response is indeed complete and successful.

http-request.html

1 Create an HTML document that embeds an external script file and contains an element in which to write and a button
```
<script type = "text/javascript" src = "http-request.js" >
</script>

<div id = "panel" >
  <button id = "btn" >Make Request</button>
</div>
```

2　Create the JavaScript file by declaring two global variables
var panel , request ;

http-request.js

3　Add an "init" function that initializes the first global variable and attaches an event-handler to the button
```
function init()
{
  panel = document.getElementById( "panel" ) ;
  var btn = document.getElementById( "btn" ) ;
  btn.onclick = doRequest ;
}
document.addEventListener( "DOMContentLoaded", init, false ) ;
```

Hot tip

Despite its name the XMLHttpRequest object can handle both plain text and XML data.

4　Above the init function define the button's event-handler
```
function doRequest()
{
  request = new XMLHttpRequest() ;
  request.open( "GET" , "data.txt" , true ) ;
  request.send( null ) ;
  request.onreadystatechange = showStatus ;
}
```

179

5　Finally, define the event-handler to show the result
```
function showStatus()
{
  if ( request.readyState === 4 )
  {
    if ( request.status === 200 )
    { panel.innerHTML += "<br>Request Succeeded" ; }
  }
}
```

Don't forget

Once this example has been run, subsequent requests will still succeed even if the data.txt file is deleted because a copy remains in the browser cache.

6　Save the script alongside the HTML document and a plain text file named "data.txt" then open the web page in a browser via HTTP and click the button to send the request

http://localhost/http-request.html

Making a HTTP Request

Make Request
Request Succeeded

100%

Using response text

When an AJAX engine makes a successful server request for text content, using an **XMLHttpRequest** object, the response automatically stores the text in the object's **responseText** property. The retrieved text can then be dynamically written into the HTML document using the DOM **innerHTML** property.

The **XMLHttpRequest** object is supported by all modern browsers but older browsers can be accommodated by testing for feature support. In particular, Internet Explorer 6 supports an alternative ActiveX object with which to make requests. This feature is named "Microsoft.XMLHTTP" and can also be tested for support. Where neither object is supported, the request call can simply return **false** to exit the function.

request-text.html

request-text.js

1. Create an HTML document that embeds an external script file and contains an element in which to write and a button
    ```
    <script type = "text/javascript" src = "request-text.js" >
    </script>
    <div id = "panel" >
      <button id = "btn" >Request Text</button>
    </div>
    ```

2. Create the JavaScript file by declaring global variables to act as a reference to the panel and a request instance
    ```
    var panel , request ;
    ```

3. Add an "init" function that initializes the first global variable and attaches an event-handler to the button
    ```
    function init()
    {
      panel = document.getElementById( "panel" ) ;
      var btn = document.getElementById( "btn" ) ;
      btn.onclick = doRequest ;
    }
    document.addEventListener( "DOMContentLoaded", init, false ) ;
    ```

4. Above the init function, start the button's event-handler function by testing for feature support
    ```
    function doRequest()
    {
      if ( XMLHttpRequest ) { request = new XMLHttpRequest() ; }
      else if ( ActiveXObject )
      { request = new ActiveXObject( "Microsoft.XMLHTTP" ) ; }
      else { return false ; }
    }
    ```

5   In the button's event-handler function block, insert
    statements to define and send a request, and to nominate
    an event-handler for the response
    request.open("GET" , "data.txt" , true) ;
    request.send(null) ;
    request.onreadystatechange = showText ;

Don't forget

The localhost domain
is the default used
by the personal web
server demonstrating all
examples in this chapter.

6   Now, define the event-handler to handle the response by
    writing the text file contents in the panel
    function showText()
    {
    ** if (request.readyState === 4)**
    ** {**
    **   if (request.status === 200)**
    **   { panel.innerHTML += "<br>"+request.responseText ; }**
    ** }**
    }

7   Create a plain text file named "data.txt" then add a simple
    line of text

data.txt

8   Save the script and text file alongside the HTML
    document then open the web page in your browser via
    HTTP and click the button to send the request

Using XML response data

Just as text retrieved by an **XMLHttpRequest** object is automatically stored in its **responseText** property, XML data retrieved by an **XMLHttpRequest** object is automatically stored in its **responseXML** property. This represents the XML document elements as "nodes" so needs additional steps to access their content. For example, all element nodes of a particular tag name can be assigned to an array variable using the **getElementsByTagName()** method of the **responseXML** property.

Each element node has a **firstChild** property, which is the text node of its content. This, in turn, has a **data** property containing the actual text content. So the **firstChild.data** property of an element node reveals the text within that XML element.

request-xml.html

request-xml.js

1 Create an HTML document that embeds an external script file and contains an element in which to write and a button
```
<script type = "text/javascript" src = "request-xml.js" >
</script>
<div id = "panel" >
  <button id = "btn" >Request XML</button>
</div>
```

2 Create the JavaScript file by declaring global variables to act as a reference to the panel and a request instance
```
var panel , request ;
```

3 Add an "init" function that initializes the first global variable and attaches an event-handler to the button
```
function init()
{
  panel = document.getElementById( "panel" ) ;
  document.getElementById( "btn" ).onclick = doRequest ;
}
document.addEventListener( "DOMContentLoaded", init, false ) ;
```

4 Above the init function, define the button's event-handler
```
function doRequest()
{
  request = new XMLHttpRequest() ;
  request.open( "GET" , "data.xml" , true ) ;
  request.send( null ) ;
  request.onreadystatechange = showXML ;
}
```

5 Now, define the event-handler to handle the response by writing the content of all XML **<name>** elements in the panel

```
function showXML()
{
  if ( ( request.readyState === 4 )
        && ( request.status === 200 ) )
  {
    var i , names =
    request.responseXML.getElementsByTagName( "name" ) ;
    for ( i = 0 ; i < names.length ; i++ )
    { panel.innerHTML += "<br>"
        + names[ i ].firstChild.data ; }
  }
}
```

Hot tip

Notice how the **&&** AND operator is used here to ensure that the response is complete and successful.

6 Create an XML document containing **<name>** elements

XML

data.xml

7 Save the script and XML file alongside the HTML document then open the web page in your browser via HTTP and click the button to send the request

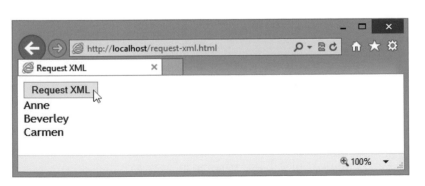

183

Creating a web application

The rest of this chapter demonstrates the creation of a web-based application that allows data on a web page to be dynamically updated without reloading the page. HTML and CSS documents produce an input form and a table with a number of empty cells. These table cells get populated with data from an XML document using the AJAX technique described in the previous example.

ajax.html

 Create an HTML document that embeds an external script file and links a CSS style sheet

```
<script type = "text/javascript" src = "request-xml.js" >
</script>
<link type = "text/css" rel = "stylesheet" href = "ajax.css" >
```

2 Next, add a table within a division of the page body

```
<div id = "databox">
<table>
<tr><td></td><td class="col">1</td>
<td class="col">2</td><td class="col">3</td>
<td class="col">4</td><td class="col">5</td>
<td class="tot">Total</td></tr>

<tr><td class="row">1</td><td id="n0"></td>
<td id="n1"></td><td id="n2"></td>
<td id="n3"></td><td id="n4"></td>
<td id="rt1" class="tot"></td></tr>

<tr><td class="row">2</td><td id="n5"></td>
<td id="n6"></td><td id="n7"></td>
<td id="n8"></td><td id="n9"></td>
<td id="rt2" class="tot"></td></tr>

<tr><td class="row">3</td><td id="n10"></td>
<td id="n11"></td><td id="n12"></td>
<td id="n13"></td><td id="n14"></td>
<td id="rt3" class="tot"></td></tr>

<tr><td class="tot">Total</td>
<td id="ct1" class="tot"></td>
<td id="ct2" class="tot"></td>
<td id="ct3" class="tot"></td>
<td id="ct4" class="tot"></td>
<td id="ct5" class="tot"></td>
<td id="gt" class="gto"></td></tr>
</table>
</div>
```

Hot tip

The empty white cells in the table body have ids "n0"–"n14", the row total cells have ids "rt1"–"rt3", the column total cells have ids "ct1"–"ct3", and the grand total cell at the bottom right has the id of "gt".

3 After the table division add a form containing two selection boxes, a text input field and a button

```html
<form action = "" ><fieldset id = "editbox" >
<legend id = "title" >Cell Editor</legend> <div>
<select id = "rownum" >
        <option selected ="selected" >Row</option>
        <option>1</option><option>2</option>
        <option>3</option></select>
<select id = "colnum" >
        <option selected = "selected">Column</option>
        <option>1</option><option>2</option>
        <option>3</option><option>4</option>
        <option>5</option></select>
New Value:
<input id = "new_value" type = "text" size = "5" value="" >
<input id = "btn" type = "button" value = "Update" >
</div></fieldset></form>
```

4 Save the HTML document then create the CSS style sheet alongside it – open the web page in your browser to see the style applied to the table and form components

ajax.css

```css
table    { text-align : center ;              }
td       { width : 50px ; height : 20px ;  }
td.col   { background : #C9E5FC ;           }
td.row   { background : #C9F2BA ;           }
td.tot   { background : #FF6600 ; color : white ; }
td.gto   { background : #FFBF23 ;                }
div#databox{ width : 360px ; padding : 5px ; margin : auto ; }
fieldset#editbox{ width : 360px ; padding : 5px ;
  margin : auto ; border : 1px solid red ; color : red ;    }
legend#title     { background : red ; color : white ;       }
```

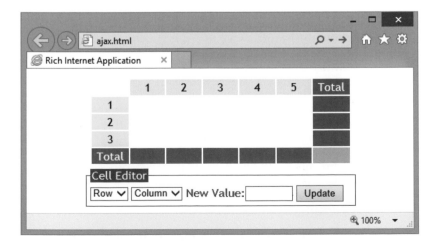

Providing application data

Having created the web application table and form on the previous page, an XML data file and JavaScript routines can be created with which to populate the table.

ajax.xml

1 Create an XML document with 15 **<num>** elements containing numeric values

```
                           ajax.xml - Notepad            –  □  ×
File  Edit  Format  View  Help
<?xml version="1.0" ?>

<root>
 <num>5.00</num>  <num>5.25</num>  <num>5.50</num>
 <num>5.75</num>  <num>6.00</num>  <num>9.50</num>
 <num>8.00</num>  <num>4.25</num>  <num>7.50</num>
 <num>3.75</num>  <num>2.25</num>  <num>8.75</num>
 <num>4.75</num>  <num>5.00</num>  <num>9.25</num>
</root>
```

ajax.js

2 Save the XML document, alongside the HTML and CSS files and then begin a JavaScript file by declaring global variables to act as an instance of an XMLHttpRequest and to store the XML data it retrieves
var request , xml ;

3 Next, add an "init" function that initializes the first global variable and nominates an event-handler for the response and the form button's click event
```
function init()
{
  if ( XMLHttpRequest )
  { request = new XMLHttpRequest() ; }
  else if ( ActiveXObject )
  { request = new ActiveXObject( "Microsoft.XMLHTTP" ) ; }
  else
  { return false ; }

  request.open( "GET" , "ajax.xml" , true ) ;
  request.send( null ) ;
  request.onreadystatechange = storeXML ;
  document.getElementById( "btn" ).onclick = update ;
}
document.addEventListener( "DOMContentLoaded", init, false ) ;
```

4 Above the init function define the response event-handler to assign XML data initializing the second global variable and call a further function to use that data

```
function storeXML()
{
  if ( ( request.readyState === 4 )
        && ( request.status === 200 ) )
  {
    xml = request.responseXML ;
    populateCells() ;
  }
}
```

5 Above the event-handler function, add the function to fill the empty table cells with XML data

```
function populateCells()
{
  var i , nums = xml.getElementsByTagName( "num" ) ;
  for ( i = 0 ; i < nums.length ; i++ )
  {
    document.getElementById( "n" + i ).innerHTML =
                            nums[ i ].firstChild.data ;
  }
}
```

6 Save the JavaScript file alongside the XML document then open the web page in your browser via HTTP to see the white cells get filled with the XML data values

Don't forget

The loop in the **populateCells()** function concatenates the letter "n" and the loop counter value to create the id of each white cell.

187

Programming the application

Once the empty white table cells have been filled with XML data, following the steps on the previous page, row totals, column totals, and a grand total can be calculated and written into the table.

ajax.js
(continued)

1 At the end of the **populateCells()** function, insert a call to a function to calculate totals
totalize() ;

2 Above the **populateCells()** function block, begin the function to calculate totals by declaring some variables

```
function totalize()
{
  var i , sum = 0 , row_number = 1 , col_number = 0 ;
  var nums = xml.getElementsByTagName( "num" ) ;
}
```

3 After the variables in the function block, insert a loop to write the total of each row in the cell at the end of each row

```
for ( i = 0 ; i < nums.length ; i++ )
{
  sum += parseFloat( nums[ i ].firstChild.data ) ;
  if ( ( i + 1 ) % 5 === 0 )
  {
    document.getElementById( "rt"+row_number ).innerHTML
                                              = sum ;
    sum = 0 ;
    row_number++;
  }
}
```

4 Next, in the function block, insert a loop to write the total of each column in the cell at the bottom of each column

```
while ( col_number !== 5 )
{
  for ( i = 0 ; i < nums.length ; i++ )
  {
    if ( i % 5 === 0 )
    {
      sum += parseFloat( nums[i+col_number].firstChild.data ) ;
    }
  }
  col_number++ ;
  document.getElementById( "ct"+col_number ).innerHTML
                                            = sum ;
  sum = 0 ;
}
```

5 Now, in the function block, insert a loop to write the grand total of all white cells in the cell at the bottom right corner of the table

```
for ( i = 0 ; i < nums.length ; i++ )
{ sum += parseFloat( nums[ i ].firstChild.data ) ; }
document.getElementById( "gt" ).innerHTML = sum ;
```

6 Save the changes and reload the web page via HTTP to see the totals get written in the table, but notice that not all totals display decimal points and two decimal places

7 Above the **totalize()** function, add a function to convert a passed numerical value into a string value and add trailing zeros where required

```
function formatted( sum )
{
  if ( sum.toString().indexOf( "." ) < 0 ) { sum += ".00" ; }
  if ( sum.toString().indexOf( "." ) ===
        ( sum.toString().length - 2 ) ) { sum += "0" ; }
  return sum ;
}
```

8 Modify the assignments to the table cells in steps 3, 4 and 5 to use the function to add trailing zeros

```
... innerHTML = formatted( sum ) ;
```

9 Save the changes once more then reload the web page in your browser via HTTP to see totals with trailing zeros

Hot tip

The number's **toString()** method converts the numeric value into a string so that string manipulation can be performed.

Running the web application

Once the total cells have been filled, following the steps on the previous page, the form button's event-handler function, which allows the user to update the table, can be added to the script.

ajax.js
(continued)

1 Just above the "init" function, begin a function that initializes three variables with form data

```
function update()
{
var row =
document.getElementById( "rownum" ).options.selectedIndex ;
var col =
document.getElementById( "colnum" ).options.selectedIndex ;
var new_value =
document.getElementById( "new_value" ).value ;
}
```

2 Next, in the function block, insert statements that validate the form data and write an advisory message if it is unacceptable

```
var panel = document.getElementById( "title" ) ;
if( row === 0 ) { panel.innerHTML= "Select a row" ; return ; }
if(col === 0) { panel.innerHTML="Select a column"; return ; }
if( !new_value ) { panel.innerHTML="Enter a value"; return ; }
if( isNaN( new_value ) )
        { panel.innerHTML = "Enter number" ; return ; }
```

Hot tip

The form legend has the id "title" and form inputs have ids of "rownum", "colnum", and "new_value".

3 Now, in the function block, enter the user's valid input value into the chosen cell then calculate and apply the new totals

```
var target = ( ( ( row - 1 ) * 5 ) + col ) -1 ;
xml.getElementsByTagName( "num" )[ target ].firstChild.data
                        = formatted( new_value ) ;
populateCells() ;
totalize() ;
```

4 Finally, in the function block, reset the form for further input

```
document.getElementById( "rownum" ).options[0].selected
                                        = true ;
document.getElementById( "colnum" ).options[0].selected
                                        =true;
document.getElementById("new_value").value = "" ;
document.getElementById("title").innerHTML = "Cell Editor" ;
```

5 Save the script alongside the HTML document then open the web page in your browser via HTTP and edit a cell value to see the totals get updated

Don't forget

When the user simply enters an integer value trailing zeros are added by the script to show two decimal places.

Summary

- AJAX is an acronym for "Asynchronous JavaScript And XML" and incorporates HTML, CSS, the DOM, JavaScript and asynchronous data retrieval by the **XMLHttpRequest** object

- Requests are sent from the web browser to the web server via HyperText Transfer Protocol, or "HTTP" for short

- Responses are also sent from the web server to the web browser via HTTP

- An AJAX engine acts as an intermediary in the request/ response cycle allowing the interface to be dynamically updated without a page reload

- The DOM's **XMLHttpRequest** object is at the core of AJAX

- Each **XMLHttpRequest** object has a **readystate** property that gets assigned numeric values at each stage of a request

- An **onreadystatechange** property nominates an event handler to process a completed response

- A successfully-completed response is signified when an **XMLHttpRequest** object's **readystate** is 4 and its **status** is 200

- When an AJAX engine successfully requests text, the content is placed in the **XMLHttpRequest** object's **responseText** property

- When an AJAX engine successfully requests XML, the content is placed in the **XMLHttpRequest** object's **responseXML** property

- XML data stored in the **responseXML** property represents the XML elements as nodes

- Each node has a **firstChild** property, which is the text node of the element, but the actual text within the XML element is contained in the **firstChild.data** property

- All XML elements of a particular name can be assigned to an array variable using the **getElementsByTagName()** method of the **XMLHttpRequest** object's **responseXML** property

13 Scripting magic

This chapter demonstrates how to employ powerful features of the latest JavaScript Application Programming Interfaces.

Dragging objects

The ability to allow the user to drag page objects and drop them onto a target is supported in HTML5 by the Drag-and-Drop API. This specifies many events that fire when the user drags an object but most important are the "dragstart", "dragover", and "drop" events. Event-handlers need to be scripted for each one of these events:

- **ondragstart event-handler** – to specify the Text data to be attached to the object being dragged, when dragging starts

- **ondragover event-handler** – to cancel the default behavior of the drop target, thereby allowing objects to be dropped on it

- **ondrop event-handler** – to define what should happen when an object gets dropped on the drop target

Additionally, the ondrop event-handler should typically ensure that the target cannot be dropped on itself.

Don't forget

Examples in this chapter are fully supported by Internet Explorer 10 (as shown) but support in other browsers may vary.

dragndrop.html

1 Create an HTML document that embeds an external script file and contains images plus an empty list

```
<script type = "text/javascript" src="dragndrop.js"> </script>
<img id="bin" src="bin.png">
<img id="Red" src="red.png">
<img id="Yellow" src="yel.png">
<img id="Green" src="grn.png">
<fieldset><legend>Folders Dropped:</legend>
<ol id="msg" ></ol></fieldset>
```

Folders Dropped:

dragndrop.js

2 Create the JavaScript file with an "init" function that gets a reference for each image element and the list element

```
function init()
{
  var bin = document.getElementById( "bin" ) ;
  var gfx = document.getElementsByTagName( "img" ) ;
  var msg = document.getElementById( "msg" ) ;
  /*  More instructions go here */
}
document.addEventListener( "DOMContentLoaded", init, false ) ;
```

3 For the ondragstart event-handler, add a loop to attach the id of the image element being dragged as Text data

```
for ( var i = 0 ; i < gfx.length ; i++ )
{
  gfx[ i ].ondragstart = function( event )
  { event.dataTransfer.setData( "Text" , this.id ) ; } ;
}
```

4 For the ondragover event-handler, cancel the default behavior of the bin – so objects can be dropped on it

```
bin.ondragover = function( event ) { return false ; } ;
```

5 For the ondrop event-handler, first get the id of the object being dropped and a reference for that image element

```
bin.ondrop = function( event )
{
  var did = event.dataTransfer.getData( "Text" ) ;
  var tag = document.getElementById( did ) ;
  /*  More instructions go here */
} ;
```

6 Next, insert an instruction to write the id of the dropped element into the list – unless it is the bin image itself

```
if ( did === "bin" ) { return false ; }
else { msg.innerHTML += "<li>" + did ; }
```

7 Finally, insert instructions to remove the dropped image element from the page and to end the drop function – then save the script alongside the HTML document and magically drag'n'drop folders into the bin

```
tag.parentNode.removeChild( tag ) ;  return false ;
```

Hot tip

Notice that the arguments to the dragstart event's **dataTransfer.setData()** method specify the data format and the actual data – in this case the "Text" format and the id of the dragged element.

195

W3C®

Discover more about the Drag-and-Drop API online at **dev.w3.org/ html5/spec/dnd.html**.

Storing information

The ability to store user data is supported in HTML5 by the excellent Web Storage API that makes storing user data a breeze. This provides a **localStorage** object, which retains stored data even after the browser has been closed, and the **sessionStorage** object, which retains stored data only until the browser gets closed. Each of these objects has identical methods to store and retrieve data. The **setItem()** method requires two arguments to specify a key and the data to be stored. For example, using the key "Name" in **localStorage.setItem("Name", "Mike")**. Stored data can then be retrieved, by specifying the key as the sole argument to the **getItem()** method, or removed by specifying the key as the sole argument to a **removeItem()** method. Additionally, all stored items can be deleted using the **clear()** method – without any arguments.

Beware

All data in **localStorage** and **sessionStorage** is stored as string values – so adding retrieved values of 5 and 7 will get concatenated as 57.

webstorage.html

webstorage.js

Don't forget

Pages must be served via HTTP (from a web server) to use Web Storage.

1. Create an HTML document that embeds an external script file and contains a fieldset with a text input and three buttons
```
<script type="text/javascript" src="webstorage.js" ></script>
<fieldset><legend id = "leg" >Enter Name</legend>
<input id = "username" type = "text" >
<button id = "store">Store Name</button>
<button id = "recall">Recall Name</button>
<button id = "remove">Remove Name</button>
</fieldset>
```

2. Create the JavaScript file with an "init" function that nominates an event-handler for each button's click event
```
function init()
{
  document.getElementById( "store" ).onclick = storeName ;
  document.getElementById( "recall" ).onclick = recallName ;
  document.getElementById("remove").onclick = removeName;
}
document.addEventListener( "DOMContentLoaded", init, false ) ;
```

3. Now create an event-handler function for the first button – to save the user data in local storage if valid
```
function storeName()
{
  var username =
    document.getElementById( "username" ).value ;
  if( username === "null" || username ==="" ) return false ;
  localStorage.setItem( "user" , username ) ;
   /*  More instructions go here */
}
```

4 Next, in the script function, insert instructions to clear the text field and display a confirmation message

```
document.getElementById( "username" ).value = "" ;
document.getElementById( "leg" ).innerHTML =
"\"" + localStorage.getItem( "user" ) + "\" is Stored" ;
```

5 Add an event-handler function for the second button – to retrieve and display the user data in local storage

```
function recallName()
{
  if ( localStorage.getItem( "user" ) === null ) return false ;
  document.getElementById( "username" ).value = "" ;
  document.getElementById( "leg" ).innerHTML =
  "Stored Name is \""+ localStorage.getItem("user") + "\"" ;
}
```

6 Finally, add an event-handler function for the third button – to remove the user data in local storage

```
function removeName()
{
  if ( localStorage.getItem( "user" ) === null ) return false ;
  document.getElementById( "leg" ).innerHTML =
  "\"" + localStorage.getItem( "user" ) + "\" is Removed" ;
  localStorage.removeItem( "user" ) ;
  document.getElementById( "username" ).value = "" ;
}
```

7 Save the script alongside the HTML document then open the web page in your browser and store a user name

8 Restart your browser and re-open this web page then push the "Recall Name" button to see the data has been magically retained – push "Remove Name" to delete it

Don't forget

Backstroke characters in this script simply escape some quote marks.

Hot tip

A shorthand alternative lets you simply tag the key onto the object name. For example, **localStorage. setItem("A","1")** can be expressed as **localStorage.A="1"** and **localStorage.getItem("A")** as **localStorage.A**.

W3C®

Discover more about the Web Storage API online at **www.w3.org/TR/ webstorage**.

Passing messages

The ability to allow plain text messages to be securely sent between documents is supported in HTML5 by the Messaging API. This is even possible when the documents are hosted on two different domains. For example, a document hosted on the local domain might include an inline frame containing a document from a different domain, which can securely send messages to each other.

To send a message to another document a reference to the receiving document's containing window is first required by the sending document. For an inline frame this is available from its **contentWindow** property. The Messaging API then provides it a **postMessage()** method that requires two arguments – to specify the message to be sent, and the target document domain. For example, **otherWindow.postMessage("Hello", "http://example.com"**).

In order to receive a message sent from another document, a message "listener" must first be added to the receiving document. This requires three arguments be supplied to that window's **addEventListener()** method – to specify it should listen for a "message" type, the event-handler function to process the message, and a boolean **false** value to indicate no further processing is required.

The message is passed to the event-handler as an "event" that has an **origin** property, containing the domain of the sending document, and a **data** property, containing the text message.

Hot tip

The HTML documents need not share the same script, but as they do **msg-send.html** is already listening for messages – so this example could be extended to allow it to receive messages sent from **msg-receive.html**.

Don't forget

Pages must be served via HTTP (from a web server) to use Messaging.

198

msg-send.html

1 Create an HTML5 document that incorporates a script, a paragraph to display the document domain, an inline frame for a remote domain, and a "Send Message" button

```
<script src = "http://localhost/msg.js" > </script>

<p id = "host" >Main Page Domain: </p>
<iframe id = "ifr" width = "450" height = "120"
  src= "http://www.example.com/msg-receive.html" >
</iframe>
<button id = "btn" >Send Message</button>
```

msg-receive.html

2 Next create an HTML document that incorporates the same script and has paragraphs to display the domain and message

```
<script src = "http://localhost/msg.js" > </script>

<p id = "host">Iframe Page Domain: </p>
<p id = "para" ></p>
```

③ Create the JavaScript file to send and receive a message

```javascript
function sendMsg()
{
  var win = document.getElementById( "ifr" ).contentWindow ;
  win.postMessage( "Message Received from: " +
          document.domain , "http://www.example.com" ) ;
}

function readMsg( event )
{
  if ( event.origin === "http://localhost" )
  document.getElementById( "para" ).innerHTML =
                                    ( event.data ) ;
}

function init()
{
  document.getElementById( "host" ).innerHTML +=
                              document.domain ;
  window.addEventListener( "message", readMsg, false ) ;
  document.getElementById( "btn" ).onclick = sendMsg ;
}
document.addEventListener( "DOMContentLoaded", init, false ) ;
```

msg.js

④ Save the first HTML document and JavaScript file on the local domain, and the second HTML document on the remote domain, then click the button to magically send a cross-document message

Don't forget

As a security precaution, cross-document messaging only succeeds when the sender correctly specifies the receiver's domain in the **postMessage()** method, and the receiver correctly verifies the sender's domain in the message's **event.origin** property.

199

W3C®

Discover more about the Messaging API online at **www.w3.org/TR/ webmessaging.**

Interacting with vectors

SVG graphics embedded in an HTML5 document maintain an XML Document Object Model (DOM) node tree of all their elements and attributes. This is separate from the HTML DOM but can be easily accessed through scripting to allow the HTML document to interact with the embedded SVG graphic.

The key to accessing the embedded XML DOM is to first create a reference object to the SVG document with a **getSVGDocument()** method. Then elements, attributes, and text in the SVG document can be addressed via the reference object.

interact.html

1 Create an HTML5 document that incorporates a script, embeds an SVG graphic, and includes a text input field and a push button in its body section

```
<script type = "text/javascript" src = "interact.js" >
</script>
<embed id = "svgDoc" src = "interact.svg"
  type = "image/svg+xml" width = "500" height = "70" >
<br> <input id = "htmTxt" size = "50" >
<button id= "htmBtn">Send To SVG Document</button>
```

interact.svg

2 Next, create the SVG graphic containing text and a circle

```
<?xml version = "1.0" encoding = "UTF-8" ?>
<svg xmlns = "http://www.w3.org/2000/svg"
  version = "1.1" width = "100%" height = "100%"
  viewBox = "0 0 500 70" preserveAspectRatio = "none" >

<text id="svgTxt" x="10" y="50" font-size="30"  fill="#F30"
        font-family="Comic Sans MS" >SVG Text</text>
<circle id = "svgBtn" cx = "460" cy = "40" r = "30"
        fill = "#F30" cursor = "pointer" /> </svg>
```

interact.js

3 Now, begin a script that creates a reference to the SVG document and elements within both documents (as global variables) when the documents have loaded

```
var svgDoc , svgTxt , svgBtn , htmTxt ;
function init()
{
  svgDoc =
  document.getElementById( "svgDoc" ).getSVGDocument() ;
  svgTxt = svgDoc.getElementById( "svgTxt" ) ;
  svgBtn = svgDoc.getElementById( "svgBtn" ) ;
  htmTxt = document.getElementById( "htmTxt" ) ;
  /* More instructions go here */
}
window.onload = init ;
```

Beware

Notice that this example gets initialized by the **window.onload** event.

4 Insert instructions to specify click event-handler functions for the HTML push button and the SVG circle

```
svgDoc.getElementById( "svgBtn" ).onclick = send2htm ;
document.getElementById( "htmBtn" ).onclick = send2svg ;
```

5 Next, add both event-handler functions to the script

```
function send2svg()
{
  svgTxt.lastChild.replaceWholeText( htmTxt.value ) ;
  htmTxt.value = "" ;
}

function send2htm()
{
  htmTxt.value = svgTxt.lastChild.wholeText ;
  svgTxt.lastChild.replaceWholeText( "SVG Text" );
}
```

6 Save all three documents then open the web page in your browser and enter some text – click the button and circle to see your text move magically between HTML and SVG

Hot tip

Notice that in the SVG (XML) DOM the actual text is contained in the **wholeText** property of the **lastChild** node of the SVG **<text>** element.

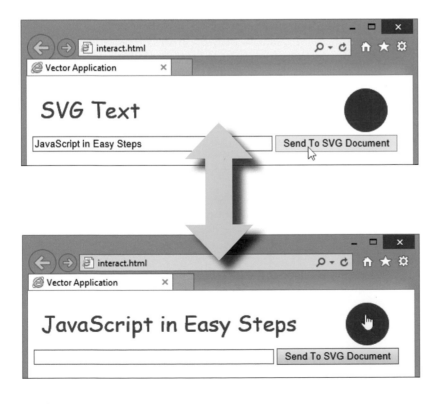

W3C®

Like HTML documents, SVG documents can also be validated by the W3C's online validator tool at **validator.w3.org**.

Locating users

The ability to pin-point the user's geographic location is supported in HTML5 by the wonderful Geolocation API. This first requests the user's consent to share location details – to send information about nearby wireless access points and the computer's IP address to, say, Google Location Services. This service returns the user's estimated latitude and longitude coordinates. Coordinates successfully retrieved can be displayed on the page and supplied to the Google Maps service to acquire a map at that location.

geolocation.html

geolocation.js

1 Create an HTML document that incorporates two scripts, and includes two fixed-size paragraphs in the body section

```
<script type="text/javascript" src="geolocation.js" >
</script> <script type = "text/javascript" src =
   "http://maps.googleapis.com/maps/api/js?sensor=true" >
</script>
<p id = "msg" style = "width:450px;height:50px" ></p>
<p id = "map" style = "width:450px;height:200px"></p>
```

2 Now, create a script with a function that attempts to seek the user location when the HTML document has loaded

```
function init()
{
  if ( navigator.geolocation )
  { document.getElementById( "msg" ).innerHTML =
        "Geolocation service is trying to find you..." ;
    navigator.geolocation.getCurrentPosition( success , fail ) ; }
  else { document.getElementById( "msg" ).innerHTML =
  "Your browser does not support Geolocation service" ; }
}
document.addEventListener( "DOMContentLoaded", init, false ) ;
```

3 Next add a function to display a message if the attempt fails

```
function fail( position )
{  document.getElementById( "msg" ).innerHTML =
   "Geolocation service cannot find you at this time." ; }
```

4 Add a success function to display the retrieved coordinates when the attempt succeeds

```
function success( position )
{
  var lat = position.coords.latitude ;
  var lng = position.coords.longitude ;
  document.getElementById( "msg" ).innerHTML =
  "Found you at...<br>Latitude: " +lat+ ", Longitude: " +lng ;
  /* More instructions go here */
}
```

5 Now, in the success function, add instructions to load a map from Google Maps – using the retrieved coordinates

```
var latlng = new google.maps.LatLng( lat , lng ) ;
var options = { zoom: 18 , center : latlng ,
        mapTypeId: google.maps.MapTypeId.ROADMAP } ;
var map = new google.maps.Map
        ( document.getElementById( "map" ) , options ) ;
var marker = new google.maps.Marker
    ( { position: latlng , map: map , title: "You are here" } ) ;
```

6 Save the HTML document and script then open the web page – agree to share to get magically pin-pointed

Don't forget

In this example the **navigator.geolocation** object provides the **getCurrentPosition()** method that must specify functions to handle success and failure. These functions must each accept a returned **position** object argument as that contains the coordinates, or error details.

203

Discover more about the Geolocation API online at **dev.w3.org/geo/api**.

Painting on canvas

In HTML5 the **<canvas>** element creates a bitmap canvas area on the page in which JavaScript can paint shapes and text using methods and properties of the Canvas 2D API. Animations can easily be created on a canvas simply by repeatedly clearing the current canvas then repainting it with shapes at a modified position faster than the human eye can detect. The fundamental components of a canvas animation script are:

- Initialize a context object and shape starting positions

- Clear the canvas, then paint shapes onto the canvas

- Calculate new shape positions for the next repaint

canvas.html

canvas.js

1 Create an HTML document that incorporates a script and includes a colored canvas area in the body section

```
<script type="text/javascript" src="canvas.js" ></script>
<canvas id = "canvas" width = "500" height = "150"
  style = "background: yellow ; border: 6px solid blue">
[Canvas Area] </canvas>
```

2 Next, create a JavaScript file that begins by declaring global variables for the context object, canvas size, XY coordinates, and direction step size

```
var ctx , cw , ch , x , y , dx , dy ;
```

3 Add a function that initializes a context object property as soon as the HTML document loads, then initializes the global variables with XY coordinates for the starting position of a "ball", its direction step size, and canvas size

```
function init()
{
  var canvas = document.getElementById( "canvas" ) ;
  if ( canvas.getContext )
  {
    ctx = canvas.getContext( "2d" ) ;
    ctx.fillStyle = "red" ;
    x = 5 , y = 44 , dx = 5 , dy = 5 ;
    cw = canvas.width ;
    ch = canvas.height ;
    /*  More instructions go here */
  }
}
document.addEventListener( "DOMContentLoaded", init, false ) ;
```

4 Now, insert an instruction to call a function that will calculate new XY coordinates every 25 milliseconds
setInterval(position , 25) ;

5 Next, add the function that calculates new XY coordinates and stores them in global variables – after it first calls a function to actually paint the ball onto the canvas
```
function position()
{
  paint() ;
  if ( ( x+dx > cw ) || ( x+dx < 0 ) ) dx = -dx ;
  if ( ( y+dy > ch ) || ( y+dy < 0 ) ) dy = -dy ;
  x += dx ;
  y += dy ;
}
```

Hot tip

Notice how the polarity of the direction step gets reversed when the ball collides with a perimeter – so it doesn't bounce right off the canvas.

6 Now, add the function that clears the canvas and actually paints the ball at the current stored XY coordinates
```
function paint( )
{
  ctx.clearRect( 0 , 0 , cw , ch ) ;
  ctx.beginPath() ;
  ctx.arc( x , y , 30 , 0 , Math.PI * 2 , true ) ;
  ctx.fill() ;
}
```

7 Save the HTML document and script then open the web page in your browser to see the animated ball magically bounce around the canvas

Discover more about the Canvas 2D API Online at **w3.org/TR/2dcontext**.

Swapping pixels

The amazing ability to manipulate the color of pixels in an image is provided in HTML5 by the Canvas 2D API, which was introduced in the previous example. The canvas context object has a **drawImage()** method that can copy a specified image onto a canvas, at specified XY coordinates. Information describing the color of each pixel on the canvas can then be stored in a "CanvasPixelArray" using the context object's **getImageData()** method. This method requires four arguments to specify the XY coordinates, width, and height, of the area to be stored.

A CanvasPixelArray object has **width**, **height**, and **data** properties. Of most interest, the **data** property is an array of the red, green, blue, and alpha components of each pixel stored in sequence. For example, with [r1, g1, b1, a1, r2, g2, b2, a2, r3, g3, b3, a3] the array elements r1, g1, b1, a1 describe the red, greeen, blue, and alpha components of the very first pixel – giving each color a numerical value in the range 0–255. Manipulating the numerical value in the array modifies the stored image data. The modified image can then be painted back onto the canvas, using the context object's **putImageData()** method to specify the array name, and the XY coordinates on the canvas at which to paint the image:

206

pixel.html

1. Create an HTML5 document that incorporates a.script, and in the body section includes a single image and a canvas – both of the same size

```
<script type = "text/javascript" src = "pixel.js"> </script>
<img id = "blue_flag" src = "blue_flag.png"
        width = "215" height = "150" alt = "Blue Flag" >
<canvas id = "canvas" width = "215" height = "150" >
        [Canvas Area]</canvas>
```

pixel.js

2. Now, create a JavaScript file to copy the image onto the canvas when the HTML document has loaded

```
function init()
{
  var canvas = document.getElementById( "canvas" ) ;
  if ( canvas.getContext )
  {
    var ctx = canvas.getContext( "2d" ) ;
    var img = document.getElementById( "blue_flag" ) ;
    ctx.drawImage( img , 0 , 0 ) ;
    /* More instructions go here */
  }
}
document.addEventListener( "DOMContentLoaded", init, false ) ;
```

③ Next, insert an instruction to read all pixels from the
canvas into a pixel array
var pixels =
      ctx.getImageData(0 , 0 , img.width , img.height) ;

④ Then, insert a loop construct to iterate through each
RGBA alpha component of the pixel array
```
for ( var i = 3 ; i < pixels.data.length ; i += 4 )
{
   /* More instructions go here */
}
```

⑤ In the loop construct, insert instructions to ignore white
pixels but change all blue pixels to red
```
if ( pixels.data[ i-2 ] !== 255 )
  {
    pixels.data[ i-1 ] = 0 ;        // Set b=0 – remove blue
    pixels.data[ i-3 ] = 255 ;      // Set r=255 – make red
  }
```

⑥ Finally, insert an instruction to paint the manipulated
pixel array onto the canvas
ctx.putImageData(pixels , 0 , 0) ;

⑦ Save the HTML document and script then open the web
page in your browser to see the modified Blue Flag image
get magically painted onto the canvas as a Red Flag

Hot tip

White has an RGB color
value of 255,255,255 so
the script tests each G
(green) color component
for the value 255 to
identify each white pixel.

207

Summary

- The Drag-and-Drop API allows the user to drag page objects and drop them onto a target within the page – by scripting **ondragstart, ondragover,** and **ondrop** event-handler functions

- The Web Storage API provides the ability to store user data – either permanently with its **localStorage** object, or temporarily until the browser gets closed with its **sessionStorage** object

- The Messaging API allows plain text messages to be sent securely between documents with its **postMessage()** method – and the documents need not be on the same domain

- Embedded SVG graphics maintain a node tree of elements so can easily be made interactive or animated by scripting – after creating a reference with the **getSVGDocument()** method

- The Geolocation API provides the ability to pin-point the user's location by estimating latitude and longitude coordinates – but only if the user consents to send information

- The Canvas 2D API provides properties and methods that allow JavaScript to paint shape and text onto a bitmap canvas area created by the HTML5 **<canvas>** element

- The Canvas 2D API can be used to manipulate pixel color via the **data** property of its CanvasPixelArray object

Index

J

K

L

214